Tide-drift Shells

Tide-drift Shells of the Monterey Bay Region

by
Hulda Hoover McLean

Revised by Frank A. Perry

Santa Cruz Museum Association

Published by the
Santa Cruz Museum Association
in cooperation with
the Waddell Creek Association

The Santa Cruz Museum Association is a nonprofit membership organization which assists the Santa Cruz City Museum of Natural History with its programs. The Museum maintains exhibits and collections and offers classes, field trips, and other activities pertaining to the natural history of the northern Monterey Bay area.

Santa Cruz Museum Association
Santa Cruz City Museum of Natural History
1305 East Cliff Drive
Santa Cruz, California 95062
408 429-3773

ISBN 0-9632480-0-6
Library of Congress Catalog Card Number 92-081082

CONTENTS

Foreward 7

Preface 9

Introduction 11

Part One: Class Gastropoda 16

Part Two: Class Pelecypoda 42

Part Three: Class Polyplacophora 63

Mysteries 65

Further Reading 67

Index 69

FOREWARD

I have long been an admirer of Hulda Hoover McLean. Her great love of nature touches all who have had the pleasure of her acquaintance, either personally or through her writings. Like Mrs. McLean, I began collecting local seashells as a child. I was in college in 1975 when her book, *Tide-drift Shells of the Waddell Beaches,* was first published, and I found it very helpful as I began to take shell collecting more seriously.

This book is a revised and expanded edition of that earlier work. I have added descriptions of a number of species so that the book, for the most part, covers the entire Monterey Bay area. I have also added the list of further reading. Most of the drawings are from the original edition and were made by the author. Additional drawings were made by Amy Mathews and me. Thanks to Kathryn Caruso, Jill Perry, Charles Prentiss, Mark Silberstein, Pat Smith, and Karen Wallingford for their help.

Frank A. Perry,
Research Associate,
Santa Cruz City Museum
of Natural History

[Mr. Dall] collected in two weeks no less than two hundred and nineteen species, which . . ., added to forty-four which have been previously reported as occurring there, but which he did not obtain, gives two hundred and sixty-three as the whole number of species of shells now known to have been found in Monterey.

Proceedings of the California
Academy of Sciences
1866

PREFACE

During my childhood, remote Santa Cruz beaches were wild, lovely, lonely places far from the path of picnickers and tourists. Wheeling gulls and racing sanderlings were my companions on daylong carnivals of wind and sun and sand and waves.

The dunes, untracked except by beach creatures, bloomed with beach asters, pink morning glory, and heliotrope-scented sand verbena. In early summer one walked the dunes carefully, watching out for plover nests. On autumn evenings one met little spotted skunks foraging for tidbits among the drifts.

The tidepools were thriving communities of tiny fish, sea flowers, scuttling crabs, brilliant nudibranches, and lacy seaweed in shades of red, green, purple, and brown. I would lie on the slippery rocks, wet from seaweed, chilled by the wind, watching tidepool pageants, too fascinated to leave, and so still that the shy shorebirds paid no heed to me.

Today, the easily accessible rocky ledges, alas, are no longer rich in life. Too many busloads of children have carried off the pools' helpless residents, to die and be discarded as maloderous mementoes of a day on the beach. Nevertheless, the tides continue to wash in and out, bringing shells, seaweed, flotsam, and small creatures trying to reestablish their ecosystems.

The dunes are stripped of flowers. Now, only during winter storms are beaches the wild lovely places where one can share the waves and dunes with wheeling gulls and racing sanderlings.

Hulda Hoover McLean

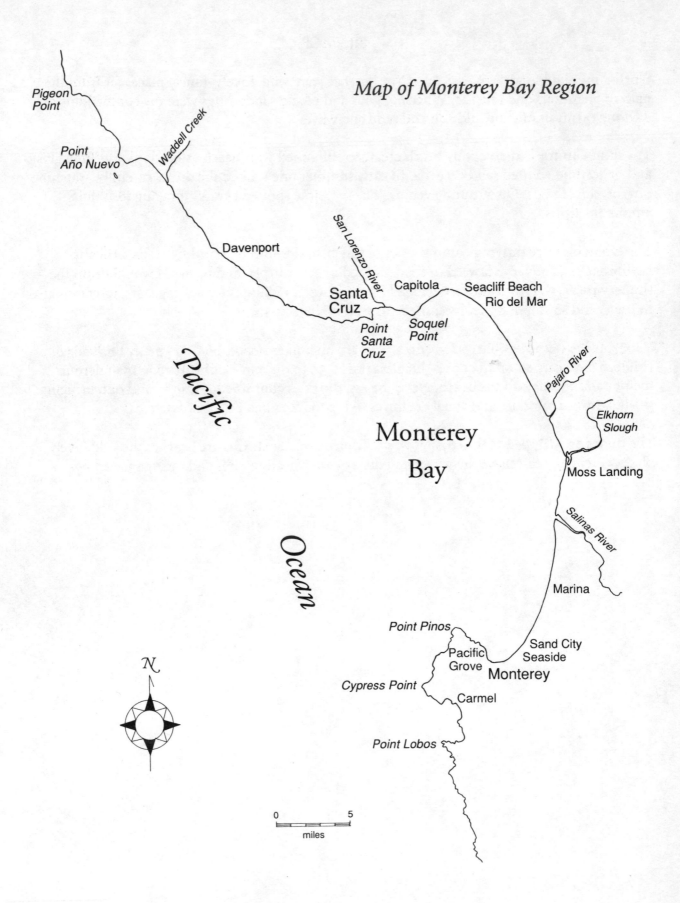

Map of Monterey Bay Region

Pigeon
Point

Point
Año Nuevo

Waddell Creek

Davenport

San Lorenzo River

Santa
Cruz

Capitola

Seacliff Beach
Rio del Mar

Point
Santa
Cruz

Soquel
Point

Pacific

Monterey
Bay

Pajaro River

Elkhorn
Slough

Moss Landing

Salinas River

Ocean

Marina

Point Pinos

Sand City
Seaside

Pacific
Grove

Cypress Point

Monterey

Carmel

Point Lobos

N

0   5
miles

PREFACE

During my childhood, remote Santa Cruz beaches were wild, lovely, lonely places far from the path of picnickers and tourists. Wheeling gulls and racing sanderlings were my companions on daylong carnivals of wind and sun and sand and waves.

The dunes, untracked except by beach creatures, bloomed with beach asters, pink morning glory, and heliotrope-scented sand verbena. In early summer one walked the dunes carefully, watching out for plover nests. On autumn evenings one met little spotted skunks foraging for tidbits among the drifts.

The tidepools were thriving communities of tiny fish, sea flowers, scuttling crabs, brilliant nudibranches, and lacy seaweed in shades of red, green, purple, and brown. I would lie on the slippery rocks, wet from seaweed, chilled by the wind, watching tidepool pageants, too fascinated to leave, and so still that the shy shorebirds paid no heed to me.

Today, the easily accessible rocky ledges, alas, are no longer rich in life. Too many busloads of children have carried off the pools' helpless residents, to die and be discarded as maloderous mementoes of a day on the beach. Nevertheless, the tides continue to wash in and out, bringing shells, seaweed, flotsam, and small creatures trying to reestablish their ecosystems.

The dunes are stripped of flowers. Now, only during winter storms are beaches the wild lovely places where one can share the waves and dunes with wheeling gulls and racing sanderlings.

Hulda Hoover McLean

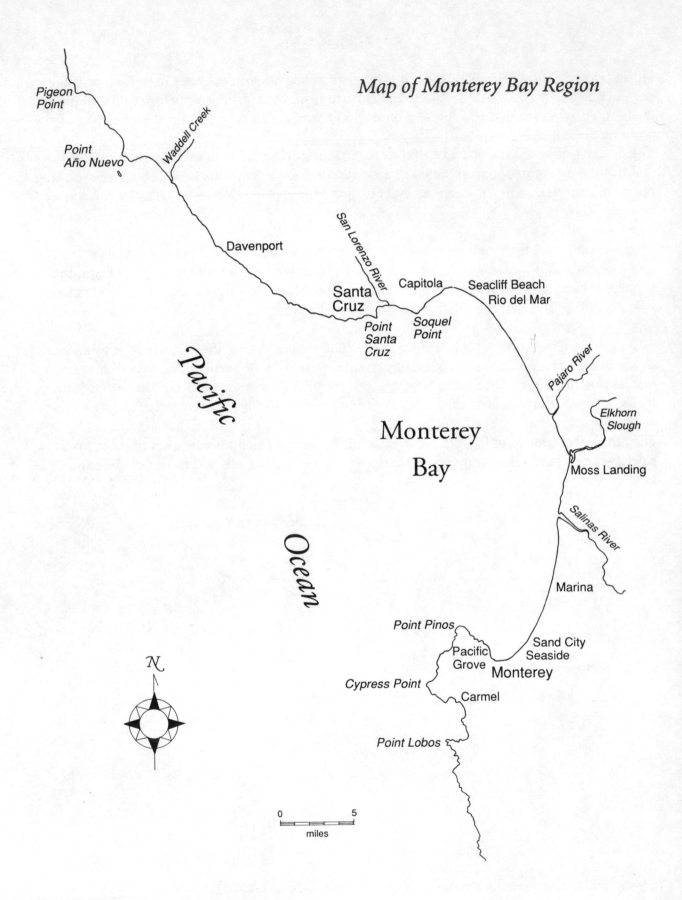

Pigeon Point

Point Año Nuevo

Waddell Creek

Davenport

San Lorenzo River

Capitola

Seacliff Beach
Rio del Mar

Santa Cruz

Point Santa Cruz

Soquel Point

Pajaro River

Pacific

Elkhorn Slough

Monterey Bay

Moss Landing

Salinas River

Ocean

Marina

Point Pinos

Sand City
Seaside

Pacific Grove

Monterey

Cypress Point

Carmel

N

Point Lobos

0   5
miles

INTRODUCTION

This book was written because the days and years of collecting on our beaches have taught me a great deal about local shells. A growing interest on the part of our young people in the natural features of the area makes the publication of my knowledge a useful project. There appears to be no other book listing all of our shells.

Here are listed, described, and illustrated all the shells I have found along the Monterey Bay area shoreline—in tidepools, on rocks, in the sand, and among the drifts. ALL the shells? Well, not quite—there are still the tiny, minute ones, only a few of which I have identified. There lies a fascinating research project for someone else in the future.

Collecting, caring for shells, identifying, and at last arranging them into your collection can bring hours of joy—working with treasures from the sea—a lifetime investment in beauty.

GEOGRAPHY

The Monterey Bay area, as shown by the accompanying map, encompasses about seventy-five miles of shoreline. Its varied coastline of rocky cliffs, coves, sandy beaches, and protected harbors and sloughs supports a rich diversity of marine life. A shell collection made from beaches along the exposed outer coast is likely to differ a good deal from one made in a cove or harbor. Many of the mollusks that live in areas sheltered from the waves are the more delicate types which cannot withstand the pounding surf.

Complex wind and current patterns produce a temperate marine climate here in central California, somewhat cooler than the waters off southern California. In fact, the mollusk life here is more like that of Oregon and Washington than the waters to the south. The coastal waters from Puget Sound south to Point Conception form what is called the Oregonian faunal province. The waters from Point Conception to the tip of Baja California form the Californian province, which is subtropical.

COLLECTING

Although all the shells in this book have come from Monterey Bay area beaches, these beaches are not the world's best collecting areas. It takes a lot of time and patience to build a collection. The best shelling is in the winter, at low tide after a storm. However, for the student, there is always something interesting. Even if there are no collectable shells, a walk along the tide drift will yield recognizable bits and pieces of fifteen to twenty species. Don't spurn them. Half the joy of collecting is in the learning process; these imperfect pieces are valuable starters—studying them will enable us to recognize and identify the perfect specimen when we finally find it. Shells, like gold, are where you find them. There is not a beach in the area where I have not found something of interest.

My collection started, as I suppose most shell collections do, in childhood with a handful, a cupful, and finally boxes full of treasures. Sadly, these were destroyed in our home fire in 1959. But now, after hundreds of sun-warmed, wind-chilled, beach hours, it is rebuilt.

Early in a collector's experience he or she will meet the "live shell vs. beach shell" controversy. Some collectors turn up their noses at beach shells and insist that no collection should contain anything which was not taken alive. But it is my firm belief that collections should be made from uninhabited, not live, shells. I don't think it is right to take live specimens, disturbing the population and needlessly terminating small miracles of life. In the case of museum or scientific collecting it may be important to examine the animal and to know exactly where and when each mollusk was living. In the case of a collector whose interest only is in the shells, insistence that it be taken alive is selfish and snobbery. Although most beach shells are, it is true, broken or faded, patience will eventually yield just as perfect a specimen dead as can be taken alive. Collecting the uninhabited shells will not disturb nature's fragile balances in tidepool and beach communities. Anyone who has seen the disappearance of mollusk populations from our beaches over the years has difficulty justifying live collecting for his or her personal collection.

In addition, live mollusks and other seashore life are protected by state laws and cannot be taken without a permit. Contact the California Department of Fish and Game for current regulations and permit procedures. Or, better still, spend your time searching for good tide-drift specimens instead. At present there are no laws restricting the taking of empty shells from most beaches except at certain state parks and reserves. Contact the local park ranger concerning collecting there.

A final word on shell collecting: don't collect on private property without asking permission from the owner. Most owners, when they understand you are not going to strip the tidepools but only collect dead shells, are happy to have you. But they are very annoyed when strangers without permission make themselves at home. How would you like strangers picnicking in your front yard?

CARING FOR YOUR SHELLS

A box of chalky, chipped shells is of no great interest to anyone. Even small children will be more interested if they follow the minimal requirements for a good collection: a label saying where and when the shell was found, a protective box lining to keep them from rattling around, and a dip into mineral oil to preserve their color and quality.

When shells are brought home from the beach they should be rinsed in fresh water. Wash and dry the shells, then dip them in a weak solution of mineral oil, or baby oil, thinned one part oil to three parts paint thinner. Never, never, never paint them with shellac or varnish. It changes their surface quality and ruins them for collections.

If you aren't going to do anything further with your shells right away, write a label numbering each shell or lot, telling the essentials, and then put them away in a plastic bag. One of the nice things about the hobby of shell collecting is that shells just sit there and wait for you to have time to identify and arrange them at leisure (unlike bird-watching where your subject often flies away without waiting to be identified, or collecting insects which must be mounted right away or they become unusable).

Keep a notebook with the shell's number and data and any extra odds and ends of information.

Were many similar ones on the beach? Which book and page contained a reference to it? How I wish I'd been more diligent with my notebook through the years!

Another no-no. Don't dip the shells in acid, as some people do to bring out the colors. Acid gives an unnatural curio-shop shine and makes the shell valueless for collections. I won't mention the horror of shell "art" and crafts.

If you mount your shells for exhibit, and if you glue them down, be sure to use the white water-soluble glue so you can unstick them if you need to. It is surprising how often that will be; either you'll want another look at the glued-down side, or you'll want to move it somewhere else, or replace it with a better specimen.

IDENTIFICATION

Identification is not the least of the collector's pleasures. It is a challenge involving research, following tantalizing clues, going to libraries and collections, and experiencing both frustration and the joy of discovery.

It is my hope that this book makes the identification of your local shells the easy part of curating your collection. The first step for the beginner is to match your shell with pictures and descriptions. As a matter of fact, I've seen some experts leaf through illustrations instead of consulting systematic keys. Many common shells with strong personalities can be readily identified through pictures. But, in using most reference books, soon you'll find you have to try to distinguish between similar pictures and to figure out baffling descriptions given in a strange vocabulary. At this point, there is no alternative; you must learn the names of the main parts of shells.

Next you'll find your field book doesn't describe all the varieties you've collected, so you'll go to the library and get more books. Horrors! Some of your best friends appear there under aliases, and some of the descriptions don't match at all! The sad truth is that names keep changing, experts have different opinions, and even the best books contain errors.

The rule is that the discoverer of a shell names it. So, every time research reveals an earlier discoverer, the name is changed to what that discoverer called it (there are exceptions to this rule). Another reason for name changes is that new knowledge may assign a mollusk to a different genus. Names are made up of the genus name, the species (and subspecies) name, and the discoverer's name (in parenthesis if the genus name he or she gave the shell has been changed). Names are in Latin so they can be used world-wide.

It is sometimes hard to be sure of an identification, and even the experts occasionally qualify their decisions. You will sometimes find the abbreviations cf. or aff. after a name. Cf. comes from the Latin *confer*, and means that the shell is similar to, and possibly identical with, the species to which it is compared. Aff. comes from the Latin *affinis*, meaning allied to or closely related. In other words, "I'm not positive but if it's not this, it's a relative." I've been tempted to put aff. after a lot of my identifications.

One thing is for sure, two experts looking over my collection would argue with each other about

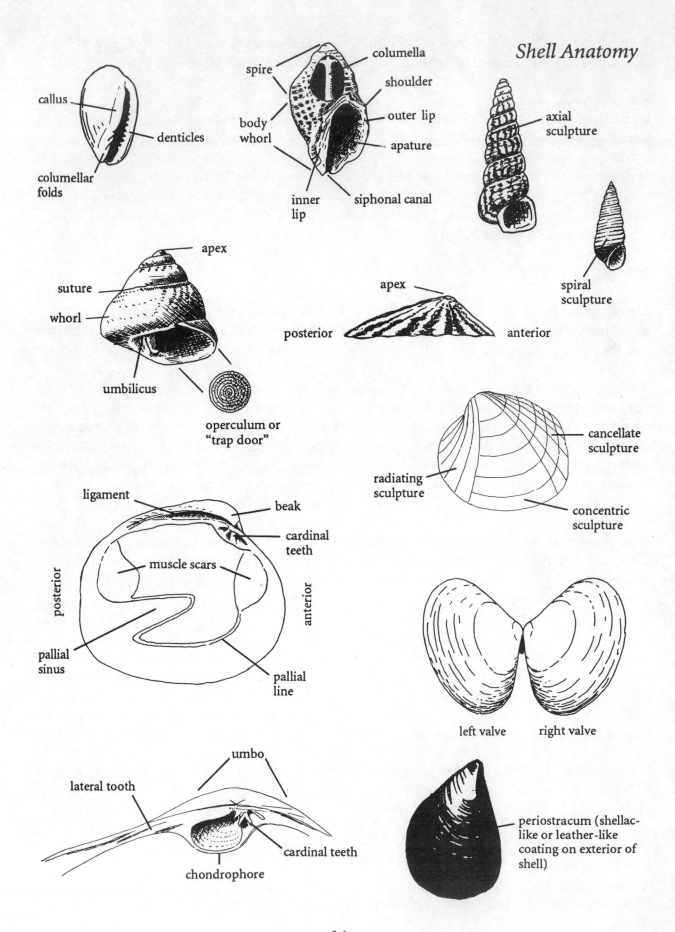

callus

denticles

columellar folds

spire

body whorl

inner lip

columella

shoulder

outer lip

apature

siphonal canal

axial sculpture

spiral sculpture

apex

suture

whorl

umbilicus

operculum or "trap door"

apex

posterior

anterior

cancellate sculpture

radiating sculpture

concentric sculpture

ligament

beak

cardinal teeth

muscle scars

posterior

anterior

pallial sinus

pallial line

left valve

right valve

umbo

lateral tooth

chondrophore

cardinal teeth

periostracum (shellac-like or leather-like coating on exterior of shell)

some of the names. And I doubt that all the names I use are the latest scientifically proper ones. However, they are the latest I have heard of. If they are more recent than those used in popular reference books, then I have tried to include both names.

Each picture in the book is a portrait of a shell in my collection, as exact as pen and black ink can render the subtle shapes and shadings of these ocean jewels. The incised line and depressions (pallial line and muscle scars) of clam shells are often only faint shadows and extremely difficult to see. In the drawings I have exaggerated them because it is sometimes very important to know what shape you are looking for; identification may depend on these faint indentations. Pen and ink cannot be an adequate substitute for photographs, especially color photographs like you'll find in some of the good reference books listed in the back. Shell sizes are given in millimeters (which you really ought to learn) and inches. You will probably find shells larger and smaller than the typical size I chose to list.

The shells are mostly arranged according to their formal classification. This book does not pretend to take the place of a good shell identification text. One needs a microscope and a detailed scientific description to make difficult identifications, and I have no intention nor qualification to give this kind of guidance.

Many experts are gracious about helping amateurs identify shells. But I know from experience what a nuisance this can be. I decided early in my collecting years that a professional's time is too valuable to waste on an amateur's ignorant questions, so I muddled along on my own most of the time. Only at the point of desperation, where nothing but an educated eye could solve the problems, have I asked for help.

Consulting another collection may make identification of problem shells easier. One of my collections is on exhibit at the Long Marine Laboratory, University of California, Santa Cruz, and the other is on display at the Rancho del Oso Nature and History Center just off Highway 1 at Waddell Creek. Other shell collections are displayed at the Santa Cruz City Museum of Natural History and at the Pacific Grove Museum of Natural History. Living examples of some of the species listed here can be viewed at the Monterey Bay Aquarium.

I was blessed with the privilege of consulting the late Myra Keen, malacologist at Stanford University, and was given access by her to the Geology Department shell collection for comparisons. Others, too, who have special knowledge of shells, have been generous with help: James McLean of the Los Angeles County Museum of Natural History, Buzz Owen of Pacific Mariculture, Eugene Coan and the late Leo Hertlein of the California Academy of Sciences, and helpful malacologists whom I met at their professional conferences.

PART ONE: CLASS GASTROPODA

ABALONES
Family Haliotidae

Abalones are the beauty queens of our local shells. They have an almost flamboyant beauty with their graceful shape and brilliantly opalescent interior. Tiny juvenile ones, half an inch long, that wash up in the tide drift are lovely enough to be set in gold and used as jewels. A graduated set of Red Abalones from one-fourth inch to ten inches makes a magnificent wall ornament. Even broken pieces add brilliant color to a bowl of pebbles or to semi-precious jewelry. Before Europeans settled this region the Indians used the abalones for bowls—they stopped up the holes with asphalt and traded them to the inland tribes. They are valued for jewelry by the Southwest Indians. Since they live attached to rocks, their shells are found on beaches near rock formations.

They are used extensively in shell "art," but I've never been able to like them, or any other shell, used as lamp bases, ash trays, or stuck together to decorate trays and boxes. That seems to me a shoddy prostitution of their beauty.

Buzz Owen of Pacific Mariculture (formerly at Pigeon Point) probably knows more than anyone else about our abalones, and he taught me almost all I know about them. Most of these abalones grow much larger than the specimens illustrated here.

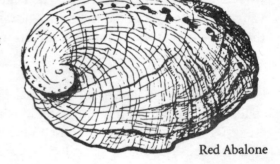
Red Abalone

The RED ABALONE, *Haliotis rufescens* Swainson, 200 mm (8") , has been the commonest on our rocks. It is rare now because it is so delicious and brings such a high price in the market. Although protected by a limited hunting season, minimum legal size, and maximum bag limit, the population has decreased until it is no longer easy to find them on a low tide— in fact, almost impossible without diving for them.

However, an occasional shell still washes up on the beach, to be added to our collection or taken home by beach-combing tourists. The Red Abalone is brick red on the outside, but sometimes the color hardly shows because the elderly ones support a garden of seaweed on their backs, as well as Rock Scallops, Pearly Monias, barnacles, a tiny piddock, sponges, and several kinds of worms. The outside red coat often makes a narrow rim around the inside, which otherwise is a brilliant opalescent, and often pinkish, mother-of-pearl. The edges of the shells are often chipped. One cause of this is rock crabs, which sometimes attack and feed on abalones.

Abalones live on rocks. They used to live up to middle tide, but now one seldom finds them even at low tide. One May morning a few years ago when my husband Chuck and I went down to an early minus tide, we saw dozens of them moving over the exposed rocks. It was a time when sand was shifting back onto the beaches and we wondered if perhaps that had disturbed them.

The largest red we ever found was ten inches. Lud McCrary, who lives just south of Waddell Creek, got one 10½ inches and four inches deep with two pounds of meat in it. He had to dive and get it out of a hidden crevice.

BLACK ABALONES, *Haliotis cracherodii* Leach, are the commonest along the coast now that the red has disappeared from rocks exposed at low tide. The Black grows to about 150 mm (6") and is easy to identify because it is the only abalone with a smooth black shell, at least on our beaches. The opalescent interior is apt to be paler and more silvery than the other varieties.

Black Abalone

The FLAT ABALONE, *Haliotis walallensis* Stearns, 150 mm (6"), is commonly confused with the Red, but it is fairly easy to distinguish the two species. The Flat is smaller, and, if the shell is held up to the light, it shows many zigzag lines. It is longer and flatter than the other varieties. Under a magnifying glass the small lines between the ridges give an almost beaded effect. Occasionally a Red will be flat and long and have some zigzag lines, specially a young one.

Flat Abalone

The PINTO ABALONE, *Haliotis kamtschatkana* Jonas, 125 mm (5"), is uncommon but still found in several locations along our beaches. It is a higher and thinner shell than the others. There are two deep trenches on the back, one above and one below the holes. It grows to be about 5 inches long. The whole shell is somewhat bumpy and the bumps show up on the inside as hollows. The name is descriptive of the sometimes splotchy coloration of red, green, gray, and orange. Inside it has a lovely pearly iridescence.

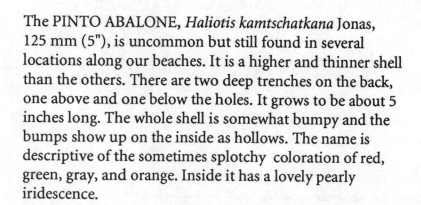

Pinto Abalone

The THREADED ABALONE, *Haliotis assimilis* Dall, 125 mm (5"), is the most beautiful of our abalones, having often a bright orange band on the outside. It has rather prominent ribs separated by a lot of finer ribs. Otherwise, it seems to be the same as the Pinto. Buzz Owen says they are the same species; that they have geographical color differences that meet on our beaches. The northern is the Pinto and the southern is the Threaded. Here there are crosses which make identification even more difficult.

Threaded Abalone

Because of the experiments in growing abalones at Pacific Mariculture, it is possible that shells of other non-indigenous varieties may show up from time to time. I once found a one-inch PINK ABALONE, *Haliotis corrugata* Gray, on our beach. It is native to southern California, and I would guess that it came from Buzz Owen's project.

LIMPETS
Families Acmaeidae, Fissurellidae, and Siphonariidae

Many reference books don't agree with each other when it comes to limpet names and descriptions; they just add to the frustration. However, James McLean of the Los Angeles County Museum of Natural History (no relation as far we know, alas) is THE authority on west coast limpets, and he was kind enough to check my identifications. So I feel confident they are correct. I gave the museum my duplicate limpet collection.

The best way to learn about limpets is to gather dozens of the shells and then separate them into piles of similar ones, while studying the pictures and descriptions. It was a great day in my life when I finally learned to distinguish between them, but I must admit that there are still—well, to be frank, sometimes they appear to be masquerading as each other. One has a choice of marking these puzzles with a question mark, or quietly putting them back on the beach. Positive identification can be made by their microscopic teeth, the radula, but if you are in the tooth-counting class of shell collectors, you are way beyond me and are reading this book for amusement rather than instruction.

In the late 1960s James McLean assigned most of our limpets that were formerly in the genus *Acmaea* to the genera *Collisella* and *Notoacmea* on the basis of their radulas. Several years ago, David Lindberg of the University of California, Berkeley, proposed that these names be changed yet again! For ease of comparison with reference books (which do not yet have the new names), McLean's names are retained here.

Of the twenty species of limpets I have identified, fifteen belong to the family Acmaeidae (the true limpets), and eight of these are especially confusing. Let's start with the confusing ones:

The RIBBED FINGER LIMPET, *Collisella digitalis* (Rathke), 25 mm (1"), is very common. It lives on rocks that are dry except at high tide; in fact, some survive on just the spray from high-tide breakers. The inside is shiny blue-white with a dark brown spot in the middle, and a black and tan border at the rim. The apex often overhangs the anterior edge and gives it its characteristic shape—the key to its identification. The grayish outside, usually deeply ridged, especially at the posterior end, is often minutely speckled, often striped or checkered, or a solid color, or mixed colors with stripes and checks.

Ribbed Finger Limpet

The MASK LIMPET, *Notoacmea persona* (Rathke), 45 mm (1¾"), is the largest of our "Acmaea" limpets (of all our limpets only the Owl is larger). It has a rounded, bulgy look which, once seen, will always be recognized. The apex is near the anterior, somewhat like the Finger Limpet, but it doesn't overhang. The inside is shiny blue-white with a brown stain in the center and a black

Mask Limpet

band around the rim. The outside color is dark brownish, speckled, or spotted, but not ridged. Two good places to see them alive are in wide shaded cracks in rocks and on the ceilings of caves.

If you can't decide what species a limpet is, it is apt to be a SHIELD LIMPET, *Collisella pelta* (Rathke), 35 mm (1⅜"). They are the most numerous on our rocks and have the widest variation of shape and color. Typically they are rather high and have the apex near center. They are shiny blue-white inside with a brown center spot, black and tan rim border. The outside can be ridged (usually) or smooth, striped, spotted, checkered, brown or black. Elderly shields are apt to be eroded and so have white apexes. They live on the upper rocks, sometimes only washed by high tides.

A dark flat limpet is more apt to be a PLATE LIMPET, *Notoacmea scutum* (Rathke), 50 mm (2"), than anything else. Although it measures larger than the Mask Limpet, it is not as tall and bulky. Inside it is shiny blue-white with a brown spot in the center and a black and tan rim border. (If the border is plain black it is probably a Fenestrate Limpet.) The outside is brown and gray, often striped or beautifully checkered. The apex is definitely toward the rear. They are found on rocks of the middle tide zone.

The FENESTRATE LIMPET, *Notoacmea fenestrata* (Reeve), 35 mm (1⅜"), is somewhat flattened and is dark brown, inside and out. The dark inside center spot is outlined in a lighter color, and the border is black. Fenestrates live low on the rocks, sometimes below the sand line.

The FILE LIMPET, *Collisella limatula* (Carpenter), 25 mm (1"), is flat and has thin, rough, file-like ribs. We seem to have two color phases here: (1) a blond one, cream and tan outside, creamy white inside with a white or tan center spot and tan rim border; and (2) a dark one, greenish gray outside, blue-white inside with a brown center-spot and a solid black rim border. They are the only limpets I have found here under loose rocks lower than, or mixed with, the lowest Finger Limpets and Plate Limpets.

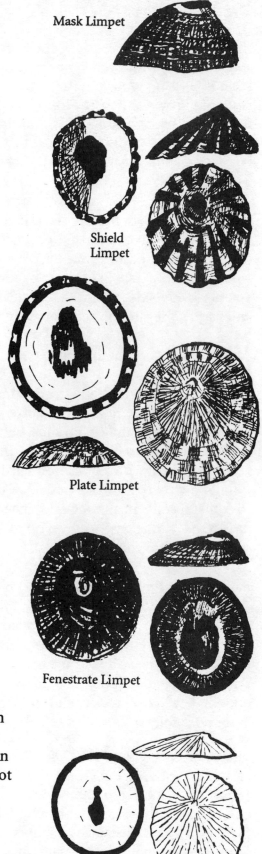

Mask Limpet

Shield Limpet

Plate Limpet

Fenestrate Limpet

File Limpet

19

The much smaller STRIPED LIMPET, *Collisella strigatella* (Carpenter), 20 mm (¾"), could be mistaken for a juvenile shell of several other species. However, the central inside spot is usually white and the outside tip is white. The inside band is black and tan, and the outside, below the white tip, is striped brown and white. Inside is shiny blue-white. It lives on exposed rocks. David Lindberg, in his book on limpets of San Francisco Bay, says that this species should be called *Collisella paradigitalis* (Fritchman).

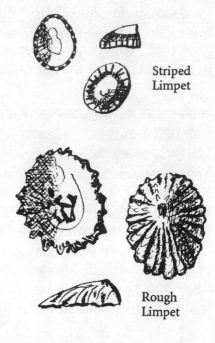

Striped Limpet

The ROUGH LIMPET, *Collisella scabra* (Gould), 25 mm (1"), is smaller than most of its relatives and is easily identified by the brown chinese-like characters in the center of the light, dull (not shiny like the others) inside. Inside, when not white, is light gray or tan, the rim border is tan and black. Outside it is apt to be flattish, ridged, green-gray and white. They live on rocks at about the high tide line.

Rough Limpet

And that takes care of the eight confusing limpets. Now for the rest of the limpets.

Our largest limpet is also in the family Acmaeidae. It is the OWL LIMPET, *Lottia gigantea* (Sowerby), 75 mm (3"). It has a bumpy gray and cream shell, but it is usually too badly eroded to see the nice pattern. Inside it is dark brown, highly polished, with a bluish-outlined, brown, owl-shaped stain in the center. It makes a shallow depression on the rock that just fits it; although it wanders around, it comes back to its "home base." It lives on rocks exposed to strong surf in the middle intertidal.

Owl Limpet

Easy to spot is the ubiquitous WHITECAP LIMPET, *Acmaea mitra* Rathke, 25 mm (1"). This is the plain white, smooth limpet so often washed up on the tidelines of the beach. Sometimes the caps are festively decorated with coralline algae in white or pink or green. Although the shells are easy to find on the beach, it is not easy to find live ones as they live on rocks below the low tide where they graze on coralline.

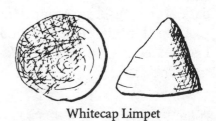

Whitecap Limpet

The UNSTABLE LIMPET, *Collisella instabilis* (Gould), 25 mm (1"), and the SEAWEED LIMPET, *Notoacmea insessa* (Hinds), 15 mm (½"), look somewhat alike, both being brown and oblong and with a rather blunt apex. However, it is easy to tell them apart. The Unstable is a shiny white inside; the Seaweed Limpet is brown inside. The Unstable rocks like a rocking chair on its convex base; the Seaweed Limpet sits tight. The Seaweed

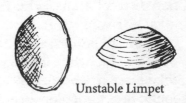

Unstable Limpet

Limpet lives on a form of kelp, *Egregia*, that looks a bit like a feather boa. It can often be found on large fronds of *Egregia* that wash ashore. The Unstable also lives attached to kelp but doesn't seem to like *Egregia*.

Seaweed Limpet

The HONEY DEW LIMPET (and that's a silly name for a mollusk) *Collisella ochracea* (Dall), 20 mm (¾"), is small, transluscent white, with brown markings. The outside pattern can be seen through on the inside. The tiny juvenile dead shells are often found stuck on the outer wall of sea anemones. Adult shells are rarely found and, when they are, are usually worn and chipped. They live among cobbles on the bottom of tide pools.

Honey Dew Limpet

The LITTLE ROCK LIMPET, *Collisella asmi* (Middendorff), 5 mm (¼"), is easily identified because it is small and black, and it lives almost exclusively attached to the shells of Black Tegula.

Little Rock Limpet

The TRIANGULAR LIMPET, *Collisella triangularis* (Carpenter), 10 mm (⅜"), is a tiny white rough limpet with a small black spot on the apex. Perhaps it has other markings, but it seems always to be coated with white coralline which hides it. It lives on coralline algae. The empty shells are mostly found adorning sea anemones or by sifting tidepool sand.

Triangular Limpet

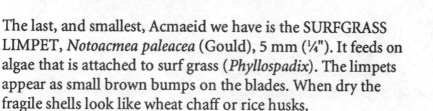

x4

The last, and smallest, Acmaeid we have is the SURFGRASS LIMPET, *Notoacmea paleacea* (Gould), 5 mm (¼"). It feeds on algae that is attached to surf grass (*Phyllospadix*). The limpets appear as small brown bumps on the blades. When dry the fragile shells look like wheat chaff or rice husks.

Surfgrass Limpet

Now we go to representatives of other limpet families:

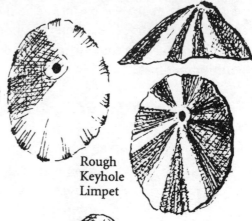

The ROUGH KEYHOLE LIMPET, *Diodora aspera* (Rathke), 35 mm (1⅜"), belongs to the family Fissurellidae, or keyhole limpets. It is the very common gray and white striped one with a hole in the apex. It lives on rocks below the low-tide line.

Rough Keyhole Limpet

Looking very much like a juvenile bleached Rough Keyhole, is the NEAT-RIB KEYHOLE LIMPET, *Diodora arnoldi* McLean, 20 mm (¾"). It can be recognized by its pale color and its shape, which is more like an Unstable Limpet than a Rough Keyhole. It lives on or under rocks below low tide.

Neat-rib Keyhole Limpet

The TWO-SPOTTED KEYHOLE, *Megatebennus bimaculatus* (Dall), 15 mm (⅝"), lives under stones, and small dead ones are often found on sea anemones. Its hole is oval and very large relative to the shell. It is cream with gray stripes. The two dark stripes on each side probably give it its name.

Two-spot Keyhole

The GIANT KEYHOLE LIMPET, *Megathura crenulata* (Sowerby), 100 mm (4"), can be distinguished by its large size. The shell is whitish, with fine radiating ribs; edge serrated. When alive, the animal's black mantle conceals much of the shell. It lives attached to rocks of the low intertidal and subtidal.

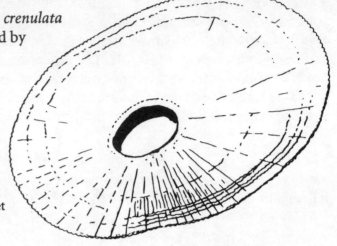

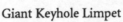
Giant Keyhole Limpet

The HOODED KEYHOLE, *Puncturella cucullata* (Gould), 25 mm (1"), is white, deeply ribbed and has a little shelf, or hood, inside the apex. It lives in deep water and is very rarely washed ashore.

Hooded Keyhole

Although not a true limpet, the SHIELD FALSELIMPET, *Williamia peltoides* (Carpenter), 10 mm (⅜"), family Siphonariidae, is limpet-shaped, so we'll include it here. It is a small, fragile shell with a hooked apex, pinkish tan inside and out, with a faint striped pattern. The shell peels off in layers, especially when dry. It lives on the undersides of rocks at low tide. Like its relative the button shell, it is a Pulmonate or air-breathing mollusk.

Shield Falselimpet

The button and hoof shells are also limpet-like in appearance and are described on page 30.

Monterey is no longer the famous collecting ground it used to be. The increasing population at and around Pacific Grove is driving away all the land shells. The deadly sewerage flowing from the various towns into Monterey Bay is killing the marine shells.

Williard M. Wood
1893

TOP SHELLS
Family Trochidae

We'll start our consideration of the snail-shaped shells with the Top Shells, Family Trochidae. These mollusks eat algae. The inside of their shells is made of mother-of-pearl (nacre).

The RIBBED TOP, *Calliostoma ligatum* (Gould), 20 mm (¾"), is the most common member of the genus *Calliostoma*. It is coffee-colored with bright blue nacre showing through at the tip and in the worn spots. This bright peacock-blue nacre and the rounded coffee-brown whorls distinguish it from its near relations. It lives on the rocks between tides. Sometimes one sees these shells in curio shops with their brown coats removed, pearly blue and defenseless-looking.

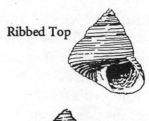

Ribbed Top

The CHANNELED TOP, *Calliostoma canaliculatum* (Lightfoot), 35 mm (1⅜"), is also fairly common. It is the largest of our Calliostomas. Its straight-sided whorls make a sharp-pointed pyramid. It is yellow-brown and its nacre is sky blue. It lives below the low-tide line.

Channeled Top

The TRI-COLORED TOP, *Calliostoma tricolor* Gabb, 20 mm (¾"), has rounded whorls of light gray-brown. Going around the whorls are narrow beaded stripes—alternate dashes of white and purplish brown. The nacre is white. It lives in deep water but is fairly common in the tide drift. This is the northern limit of its range.

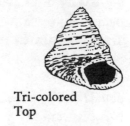

Tri-colored Top

The GLORIOUS TOP, *Calliostoma gloriosum* Dall, 20 mm (¾"), is uncommon here. In shape it is half way between the rounded Ribbed Top and the straight-sided Channeled Top. The color is tea-brown or gray, spotted with lighter and darker brown. The nacre is light and may be pinkish. How it got its "glorious" name is a mystery—I consider it the least beautiful of the group. This species was first named from a specimen collected on the beach at Capitola in the 1860s, and it still occasionally washes ashore there. It lives on rocks offshore.

Glorious Top

But, ah! The rarely found PURPLE RINGED TOP, *Calliostoma annulatum* (Lightfoot), 20 mm (¾"), is a yellow or apricot shell beaded with stripes of improbable violet; it is a jewel in any collection. It lives offshore on the blades of kelp.

Purple Ringed Top

Another rarely found gem is the GRANULOSE TOP, *Calliostoma supragranosum* Carpenter, 8 mm (⁵⁄₁₆"). It is a small, brownish top with spiral ridges and a more pronounced shoulder than the other species. The fine spiral ridges have a beaded appearance on the early whorls.

Granulose Top

Next we'll consider our Tegulas, those sturdy snail shells so popular as homes for hermit crabs.

The omnipresent BLACK TEGULA (which is purple-gray when dry), *Tegula funebralis* (A. Adams), reaches a large, lumpy 40 mm (1½") across and may be 25 years old, but is more apt to be smaller, 20-25 mm (¾ to 1"). The apex is usually eroded and orange-colored. The Black Tegula often wears small black limpets, *Collisella asmi*, on its back, sometimes so many that they seem to impede the snail's slow progress over the rocks and sand. Black Tegula is considered a fine food, but it is such a slow-growing snail that the population would not long survive gourmet enthusiasm. It lives in crevices of rocks exposed at high tide.

Black Tegula

Not as plentiful on our rocks and tidepools as the Black Tegula, but still numerous, is the BROWN TEGULA, *Tegula brunnea* (Philippi). It also occasionally grows to a lumpy 40 mm (1½") but is usually much smaller. It boasts rich shades of brown with nacre showing through in worn areas. It is distinguished from the other three brownish tegulas by not having an umbilical hole in the bottom, just a pearly depression. They mingle with the Black Tegulas but are more numerous a little lower on the rocks. The Hooked Slipper likes to live piggyback on the Brown Tegula shell.

Brown Tegula

The DUSKY TEGULA, *Tegula pulligo* (Gmelin), 20 mm (¾"), is shaped like a young Brown Tegula, but has a deep umbilical hole with a keel edge around it. It also is sometimes marked with dusky spots. It is uncommon on our beaches.

Dusky Tegula

Another less common Tegula here is the MONTEREY TOP, *Tegula montereyi* (Kiener). It is the biggest in the family, often 45 mm (1¾") across. It is the only straight-sided pyramid among our tegulas. It has a deep, unkeeled, umbilical hole in the bottom. Recognizable pieces of shell are fairly often found, but good specimens are scarce. It lives on off-shore kelp. It is usually tan, but sometimes orange or gray.

Monterey Top

One of the smaller members of the Top Shell family found in our tide drift is the PUPPET MARGARITE, *Margarites pupillus* (Gould), 8 mm (⁵⁄₁₆"), pinkish tan, with a tiny umbilical hole. It lives on the low-tide rocks.

Puppet Margarite

Last, and perhaps least, are the LIRULARIA TOP SHELLS. I
hesitate to mention them because it takes a strong magnifying glass,
or better yet, a microscope, to see their distiguishing features. Too
bad. Were they ten times larger, they would make spectacular
additions to any collection. There are several species including
Lirularia funiculata (Carpenter), *Lirularia parcipicta* (Carpenter),
and *Lirularia succincta* (Carpenter). All measure 3-5 mm (³⁄₁₆")
high. Their shells are a mottled brown and white with spiral ridges.

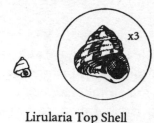

Lirularia Top Shell

TURBANS
Family Turbinidae

Turbans are closely related to Top Shells but their operculum or "trap door" is calcareous instead
of horny.

The RED TURBAN, *Astraea gibberosa* (Dillwyn), is a coarsely
ribbed brick red pyramid, sometimes 75 mm (3") or more
across the bottom. Lumpy red spiral cords make
identification, even of broken bits, easy. This, like
the Monterey Top, is rarely found in good
condition, dead or alive; large ones are invari-
ably chipped and scarred. They live on the
rocks at low tide on the outer coast.

Red Turban

The two tiny representatives of this family are the Dwarf
Turbans, 5 mm (¼"). The DARK DWARF TURBAN,
Homalopoma luridum (Dall), is dark gray; and CARPENTER'S
DWARF TURBAN, *Homalopoma carpenteri* (Pilsbry), is brick red.
They might be confused with the Puppet Margarite, which is of similar shape
and size, but are easily distinguished by color and the fact that they have
no umbilical hole. Some experts regard these two species as synonyms, the
former name being used. We find them under tidepool rocks on the
Monterey Peninsula and on the exposed coast north of Santa Cruz.

Dwarf Turban

PHEASANT SHELLS
Family Phasianellidae

The PHEASANT SHELLS are tiny, brilliantly colored and beautifully
marked little snails, but it takes a magnifying glass to appreciate their
patterns. If they were larger, they would be our most beautiful shell of all.
Our member of the family is *Tricolia pulloides* (Carpenter), 5 mm (¼").
Each shell has a different pattern, red with black and white dots, pearl gray
with red zigzag lines, red banded with gray. It lives attached to surf grass,
but the empty shells are frequently found decorating sea anemones.

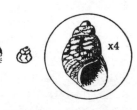

Pheasant Shell

25

CHINK SHELLS
Family Lacunidae

We seem to have at least three varieties of CHINK SHELLS. They are named for the shape of their umbilical slit which is a narrow chink or incised line on their bottoms. Most of these shells are so small it takes a magnifying glass to see their distinguishing marks. My advice is to collect a lot of them and then, some rainy day, settle down with a good light and a magnifying glass and separate them into little piles of look-alikes. You may find we have more species than I've had time, patience, eyesight, or knowledge to distinguish. Deciding just which is which is going to be difficult because reference books have contradictory descriptions of the members of this family.

The largest we have is the CARINATE CHINK SHELL, *Lacuna porrecta* Carpenter, 15 mm (½"). It is yellowish brown and has no markings on it. It lives on kelp and is fairly common.

Carinate
Chink Shell

The ONE-BANDED LACUNA, *Lacuna unifasciata* Carpenter, 5 mm (¼"), is tan and usually has a darker band around it. It has a distinctively narrow shell, relatively taller than either of the other species. It lives on eel grass and is very common.

One-banded
Lacuna

The VARIEGATED CHINK SHELL, *Lacuna marmorata* Dall, 3 mm (⅛"), is a short, round little snail, dark brown with white markings and a white band around the bottom. It lives on eel grass and is very common.

Variegated
Chink Shell

PERIWINKLES
Family Littorinidae

Periwinkles live so far up the rocks it is hard to see how they survive between high tides. They feed on algae, yet the rocks don't seem to have any algae on them.

CHECKERED PERIWINKLE, *Littorina scutulata* Gould, 10 mm (⅜"), is a pointed and highly polished shell, and although most of the shells on the rocks will be gray, many will have patterns. Each pattern is different. They may be black with white dashes, tan with gray herringbone patterned bands, gray with black and white squares, white with brown and black checks, ad infinitum. The inside is purplish. Empty shells do not often wash up on the beach, so you may have to just enjoy looking at the live ones. They live abundantly on rocks, specially in crevices, at high tide line or above.

Checkered
Periwinkle

The ERODED PERIWINKLE, *Littorina keenae* Rosewater (formerly *Littorina planaxis* Philippi), 15 mm (½"), is larger and fatter than its cousin, the Checkered Periwinkle, and occasionally, but not often, is patterned in spots or stripes or bands. Usually it is rough and grayish. It cannot be confused with other shells as it has a peculiar flat columnella

Eroded
Periwinkle

behind the inner lip, and a thin white line inside the base of the outer lip. It lives on rocks, often above the high tide line, where it must depend on ocean spray for moisture.

ALVINIA AND BARLEEIA SHELLS
Family Rissoidae

Although I have not included many of the minute species, I include these because they are fairly common in some areas and illustrate just how small some mollusks can be. They can be found by examining gravel samples with a hand lens or low-power microscope. They have no common name and are not included in most shell books.

Alvinia compacta (Carpenter), 2.5 mm (¹⁄₁₆"), grows to be about the size of a pin head. Vertical and spiral grooves give the brownish shell a cross-hatched sculpture.

Alvinia compacta

Barleeia acuta (Carpenter), 3-4 mm (⅛"), is smooth with flattened whorls and an oval aperture; yellowish or brown with darker brown mottling.

Additional species of *Alvinia* and *Barleeia* occur along our coast. Some of the references in the back of the book can be used to learn more about these.

Barleeia acuta

WORM SHELLS
Family Vermetidae

Walking the tide-line, we see many worm casings. The most striking of these is not a worm at all, but a mollusk, the SCALED WORM SHELL, *Serpulorbis squamigerus* (Carpenter). It measures 20 mm (¾") in diameter and is a large china-like shell, one with strong longitudinal scaly ridges. It is a snail shell whose whorls don't form a snail shape but are coiled in masses on rocks. After storms one can sometimes find them with the piles of seaweed. They are creamy white.

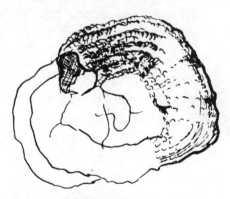

Scaled Worm Shell

A coiled worm shell rather similar to the last, but smaller and without ridges, is not a mollusk but is the calcarous shell of a polychaete worm, family Serpulidae. And, while we are talking about worm shells and polychaetes, we might as well mention the ABALONE WORM, the thin parchment-like worm that lives attached to Red Abalone shells. There is also the DIOPATRA WORM, which has a wrinkled parchment-skin tube, covered with attached bits of shells and seaweed and pebbles. It is common; sometimes the tide line is littered with them.

HORN SHELLS
Families Potamididae, Cerithiidae, and Cerithiopsidae

We have two large and many small species of horn shells.

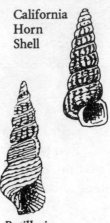

California
Horn
Shell

The CALIFORNIA HORN SHELL, *Cerithidea californica* (Haldeman), 35 mm (1⅜"), family Potamididae, is somewhat of a mystery shell. Shell books only list it from the intertidal mudflats of bays and estuaries, yet water-worn shells frequently wash up on the beaches near Waddell Creek, Capitola, and probably elsewhere too. I can only assume that it also lives offshore. It is tan or brown with low axial ridges.

Another horn shell, *Batillaria attramentaria* (Sowerby), 35 mm (1⅜"), is abundant on the mudflats of Elkhorn Slough, particularly near Jetty Road. In some places the shells are so thick that you can hardly see the mud. These detritus feeders were accidentally introduced with Japanese oysters around 1930.

Batillaria attramentaria

Giant Bittium

The GIANT BITTIUM, *Bittium eschrichtii* (Middendorff), 18 mm (¾"), family Cerithiidae, isn't much of a giant, being very slender and not very tall. It is brown or gray, with light bands and a white inner lip. It lives under rocks at low tide. I find the empty shells in fine gravel or decorating sea anemones.

*Bittium
attenuatum*

Another species, *Bittium attenuatum* Carpenter, 9 mm (⅜"), is common in beach drift near Capitola. Color variable; from brown to tan, sometimes with white bands, or almost entirely white.

Very occasionally, when sifting fine tide-drift odds and ends, I find MINIATURE HORN SHELLS of the genus *Cerithiopsis*, 3 to 6 mm (¼") high. They are shiny chocolate brown with beaded cords around each flattened whorl. Eleven species have been reported from the Monterey Bay area, six or seven from the intertidal. Don't try to sort out the different kinds, you'll go nuts.

Miniature
Horn Shell

*Metaxia
convexa*

Within the same family, the Cerithiopsidae, is the more easily recognizable *Metaxia convexa* (Carpenter), 5 mm (¼"). It is brown with a beaded sculpture like *Cerithiopsis*, but the whorls are much more convex.

Seila montereyensis Bartsch is another small horn shell, dark brown in color. Its unusual sculpture of three spiral cords per whorl makes it impossible to confuse with any other local species. It is big for the family, reaching a whopping 14 mm (½").

Seila montereyensis

TRIPHORA SHELLS
Family Triphoridae

The SAN PEDRO TRIPHORA, *Triphora pedroana* Bartsch, 8 mm (⁵⁄₁₆"), is unique among our tide-drift shells in that it is sinistrally coiled or "left-handed." When viewed from above, the shell spirals counter clockwise instead of the usual clockwise. It is brown with a beaded sculpture similar to *Cerithiopsis*.

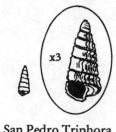

San Pedro Triphora

WENTLETRAPS
Family Epitoniidae

Wentletraps are among the most exquisite of shells; tall, slender, white, beautifully sculptured—and carnivorous. I am told that some large species were so valuable in the early nineteenth century that Chinese craftsmen made exquisite counterfeit copies from rice flour.

The CHACE WENTLETRAP, *Opalia chacei* Strong, 20 mm (¾"), is glistening white. In spite of its delicate appearance, it is a tough shell and usually found in perfect condition. It is not uncommon in our tidepools where it may be alive, or dead—often inhabited by a small hermit crab. If the *Opalia* is taken alive it is hard to remove the inhabitant, who puts out a deep purple dye when hurt. It is thought that the purple dye may be used as an anaesthetic to relax its prey.

Chace Wentletrap

The TINTED WENTLETRAP, *Epitonium tinctum* (Carpenter), up to 15 mm (½"). These exquisite tiny shells, often only ¹⁄₁₆", make one marvel at the works of the Creator. They are white or faintly tinged with tan or gray. They are commonly found as adornments on the outside of sea anemones. They stick their proboscis through the outer wall of the anemone and suck out the juices. The ones we find there are usually empty shells so perhaps the anemones fight back. The outer layer of the anemone is armed with barbed stinging cells (nematocysts) that can catch and hold prey.

Tinted Wentletrap

OBELISK SHELLS
Family Eulimidae

The only common members of this family on our beaches belong to the genus *Balcis*, height to 12 mm (½"). They are small, high-spiraled, whitish shells with flattened whorls and a shiny, glassy appearance. You should probably just label them "*Balcis* species," unless you are willing to wade through the technical literature to try to identify the separate species.

Balcis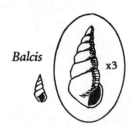

HOOF SHELLS, BUTTON SHELLS, AND SLIPPERS
Families Hipponicidae, Trimusculidae, and Calyptraeidae

HOOF SHELLS, BUTTON SHELLS and SLIPPERS are the kinds that I called "thimble shells," and wore them on my fingers, when I was a little girl beachcombing the tide drift.

The WHITE HOOF SHELL, *Hipponix tumens* Carpenter, 10 mm (⅜") high, was the best thimble. It looks like a small wilted WHITE CAP LIMPET with its drooping apex and wrinkled surface. It has varied shapes as it adapts to fit the rocks or dead shells on which it grows below the tide line. Hoof shells all have a horseshoe-shaped muscle scar which probably gave them their name. They live on organic scraps.

White Hoof Shell

The FLAT HOOF SHELL, *Hipponix cranioides* Carpenter, 10 mm (⅜") across, has a more centered apex, often with pronounced concentric rings around it. The occasionally frilled specimens may possibly be another species, *Hipponix serratus* Carpenter. Both are dingy white.

Flat Hoof Shell

BUTTON SHELLS, *Trimusculus reticulatus* (Sowerby), 10-20 mm (⅜ to ¾") across, look a good deal like the Flat Hoof Shell and have similar scars, but they are nicely sculptured with radial concentric lines. They live on rocks, like a limpet, often under ledges, at the low tide line. This shell belongs to the subclass that breathes air—a somewhat difficult feat, I should think, at high tide. It is dingy white.

Button Shell

We have four of the slipper shells, family Calyptraeidae.

The most common is the WESTERN WHITE SLIPPER, *Crepidula nummaria* Gould, 40 mm (1½"). Because it fits itself into holes and crevices, it comes in a variety of shapes. But, given room to grow freely, it is a beautiful shell with a nice round shape. It is glossy white inside and dull white outside, except when covered with a wrinkled light brown skin or periostracum, which has usually worn off the tide-drift specimens.

Western White Slipper

The THIN WHITE SLIPPER, *Crepidula perforans* (Valenciennes), is sometimes 40 mm (1½") long. It really looks like a slipper, narrow with a pointed wrinkled toe. These folds in the toe distinguish it from long and thin versions of the Western White Slipper.

Thin White Slipper

The HOOKED SLIPPER, *Crepidula adunca* Sowerby, 20 mm (¾"), is also common here. It varies from a light tea-colored delicate shell to a dark chocolate-colored tough one. Its platform is white and extends over about a third of the shell. It starts life as a male, then is

Hooked Slipper

bisexual, and then becomes a female. It lives on rocks or other shells and often piles up, one on top of another.

The ATLANTIC SLIPPER, *Crepidula fornicata* Linnaeus, 35 mm (1⅜"), has the same varied sex life as the hooked slipper. It is bigger and is streaked brown and white. A white platform extends over about half of the shell. It has been introduced from the Atlantic. Many introduced shells have had a ride on the keels of ships, and others come with imported oysters.

Atlantic Slipper

The PACIFIC HALF SLIPPER, *Crepipatella lingulata* (Gould), 20 mm (¾") across, can be a lovely pink and white shell but is usually white streaked with brown. Its platform is only connected on one side. It usually lives attached to other shells.

Pacific Half Slipper

MOON SHELLS
Family Naticidae

LEWIS' MOON SHELL, *Polinices lewisii* (Gould). We only occasionally find a large fat Moon Shell, 90 mm (3½") high, on the beach, but the small young ones, an inch or less, are common. They are usually a pale yellow tan with darker tan or gray band under the suture. They live under the sand at low tide, often revealing themselves by a hump in the sand. They are carnivorous as well as scavengers, and are responsible for some of the neat countersunk holes we often find in beach shells. They don't discriminate between their own species and others in their diet.

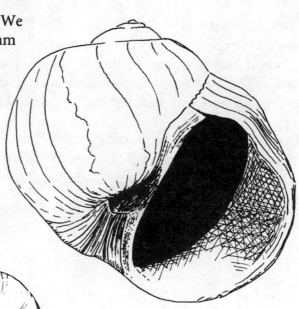

Lewis' Moon Snail

WIDE-MOUTHED SNAILS
Family Lamellariidae

The EAR SHELL, *Lamellaria rhombica* Dall, 12 mm (½"), is a fragile shell, pure shiny opaque white, rare and lovely. It is shaped somewhat like a small abalone without holes.

Ear Shell

VELVET SHELLS
Family Velutinidae

The VELVET SHELL, *Velutina* cf. *V. velutina* (Müller), 5 mm (¼"), is fragile and transparent, covered with an amber velvet skin, or periostracum. It, too, resembles a tiny fat baby abalone, without holes. If you want to find one, you'll have to lie on the wet anemone-covered rocks at low tide and peer into tidepools. It is said to live offshore in deep water, but if so, why do I only find the shells in tidepool sand?

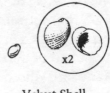

Velvet Shell

SEA BUTTONS
Family Triviidae

"Sea Button" is a confusing common name for this family. The individuals of our species are not called buttons, while our BUTTON SHELL, *Trimusculus reticulatus*, is of a different family altogether. Our two members of the family Triviidae are not rare, but are uncommon enough and pretty enough so that finding one makes the day worthwhile.

The CALIFORNIA TRIVIA, *Trivia californiana* (Gray), 10 mm (⅜"), is a lovely little lavender-gray or brownish shell, looking like a tiny ribbed cowry. If it knew its name I should think it would resent being called "trivia." Small it may be, but not trivial. It lives on seaweed and its body is a gorgeous red color. Beach gravels are a good place to look for these shells.

California Trivia

The APPLE SEED, *Erato vitellina* Hinds, 20 mm (¾"), is rose-brown and plump, looking like a small cowry with a blunt spire. Although not highly polished, it has a soft shiny glow. Contrary to its name, it is much larger than an apple seed. It lives on kelp.

Apple Seed

TRITONS
Family Cymatiidae

Our only Triton is the HAIRY TRITON, *Fusitriton oregonensis* (Redfield), 150 mm (6"), and I doubt that these large shells live on our immediate reefs because only a few times have I found, south of Año Nuevo, the broken but identifiable shells. The ones I have found are bleached white, with no trace of the shaggy hair (periostracum), which gives the shell its name. They live in deep water.

Hairy Triton

ROCK SHELLS
Family Muricidae

World wide, the family Muricidae contains some of the fanciest of shells, the Murexes. They vary in size from huge to very small, and from plain snail shells to ruffled beauties. They are carnivorous.

We come now to the queen of our shells, the lovely LEAFY HORNMOUTH, *Ceratostoma foliatum* (Gmelin), 75 mm (3"). Why doesn't it have a name nice enough to match its beauty? Frilled Rock Shell or Winged Ceratostoma, for instance, would be much more appropriate. At its best it is a beautifully frilled shell with wide bands of brown and white. It has various color phases from snowy white through tan to dark brown, with or without bands and frills. It lives on the rocks at low tide and is very plentiful in outer-coast beach-drift.

Leafy Hornmouth

The WINGED ROCK SHELL, *Pteropurpura macroptera* (Deshayes), 50 mm (2"), looks like a slender Leafy Hornmouth but is rather easily distinguished by its smooth whorls between the wings (the Leafy Hornmouth whorls are always definitely ridged). Its color is pinkish brown with a faintly violet cast. It lives in deep water and is seldom washed ashore.

Winged Rock Shell

Now we'll consider the Dwarf Rock Shells. They are very confusing, not only within their own family, but with small shells of similar shapes in other families. A bag full of Rock Shells, Amphissas, and small Dog Whelks presents a formidable (but nevertheless pleasurable) task of sorting and identifying. Our Dwarf Rock Shells don't exactly fit the descriptions given in reference books, but because these shells are apt to vary in shape and color according to locality, I've identified their probable species. Later we may find that we have additional species or subspecies.

The FILE DWARF ROCK SHELL, *Ocenebra sclera* Dall, 30 mm (1¼"), is a medium-sized attractive shell. Well-named, the rough file-like feel of its shell is an outstanding feature of both this and *O. circumtexta*. It has six or seven prominent axial ribs per whorl. It is yellow-gray and has many narrow circling grooves that are dark brown. It is not uncommon here. I consider it a close relative of *Ocenebra foveolata* (Hinds), the name used in many reference books. However, some references list *O. sclera* as a synonym for *O. lurida*.

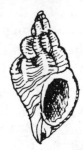
File Dwarf Rock Shell

The CIRCLED DWARF ROCK SHELL, *Ocenebra circumtexta* Stearns, 20 mm (¾"), differs from *O. sclera* in being a little fatter and in having more axial ribs, 7 to 9. It is basically white, usually with two wide brown bands on the body whorl interrupted by the axial ribs.

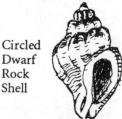
Circled Dwarf Rock Shell

The LURID DWARF ROCK SHELL, *Ocenebra lurida* (Middendorff),
15 mm (½"), may be yellow, tan, or bright orange with numerous fine
spiral grooves and weakly developed axial ribs. Its dark brown
periostracum is usually pretty well worn off in tide-drift specimens.
Common in some areas.

Lurid Dwarf
Rock Shell

The two smallest Dwarf Rock Shells are especially confusing. There may, as a matter of fact, be more than two
species involved. However, I classify the heavily axially-
ribbed, and knobby-shouldered ones as the BETA ROCK
SHELL, *Ocenebra beta* (Dall), 10-15 mm (½"). It is tan,
sometimes with a yellow stripe. I classify the ones with less
heavy axial ribs and no shoulder knobs as CARPENTER'S
ROCK SHELL, *Ocenebra interfossa* Carpenter, 10-12 mm
(⅜"), same colors as *O. beta*.

Beta
Rock Shell

Carpenter's
Rock Shell

Some books say that *O. atropurpurea* Carpenter is the same shell as *O. interfossa* which simplifies
things a bit because I had difficulty deciding which ours is. Perhaps someday a book will come
out that will straighten out all these rock shells and we'll find out how good my guesses are. In the
meantime, if you find all this hopelessly confusing, label them DWARF ROCK SHELLS, *Ocenebra*
species.

DYE SHELLS
Family Thaididae

Dye shells secrete colored fluid—red, green or purple. The royal Tyrian purple of ancient civiliza-
tions was made from a snail of this family. But I've never seen any sign of colored secretions in
our dye shells—the only mollusk dye I have experienced is from the *Opalia*.

Our largest in the family is the FRILLED DOGWINKLE,
Nucella lamellosa (Gmelin), to 75 mm (3"). It is a very handsome heavy shell that comes in several shapes and colors. At its
handsomest, it is strongly ridged both axially and radially (up
and down and around) and is orange, banded with white. The
shell also comes in white or yellow or brown, with or without
bands, and with or without ridges, but always with a toothed
and porcelain-like aperture. It lives on the intertidal rocks and
is a common shell in the tide drift along the coast near Waddell
and Scott creeks. It is very rare in more protected areas such as
near Santa Cruz. This and our other species of *Nucella* were
formerly placed in the genus *Thais*.

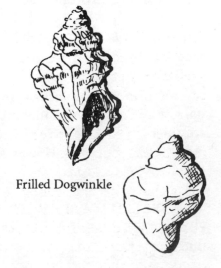

Frilled Dogwinkle

Try saying "Dogwinkle, Dog Whelk, and Wentletrap" rapidly!

One of the most numerous rock-living shells is the EMARGINATE DOGWINKLE, *Nucella emarginata* (Deshayes), 20 mm (¾"). Although it is usually inconspicuously rough and grayish on the rocks it resembles, it can be as handsome as its big cousin the Frilled Dogwinkle. Sometimes it is conspicuously black and white striped, or shiny black, or pearl gray, or even, when young, bright orange; these color phases, along with its purple columella (inner wall) are strikingly lovely. It lives on rocks and in crevices exposed at middle tide. It is a voracious carnivore and cannibal. It is especially abundant on surf-pounded rocks. I wonder why a shell so common on rocks is so seldom found in the tide drift.

Emarginate Dogwinkle

The CHANNELED DOGWINKLE, *Nucella canaliculata* (Duclos), 25 mm (1"), is a bit like the Emarginate, but tougher and taller with spiral cords. It is banded in brown and tan and white. It lives on rocks in somewhat more protected sites than the *N. emarginata*. Both are fond of mussel beds.

Channeled Dogwinkle

The ANGULAR UNICORN, *Acanthina spirata* (de Blainville), 30 mm (1¼"), is a brown or gray tweedy looking shell with a pointed tooth sticking out of the outer lip. It is colored by numerous discontinuous dark spiral lines. It is carnivorous and is often found on rocks among mussels or nestled next to sea anemones. A common shell in the tide drift.

Angular Unicorn

Closely related is the SPOTTED UNICORN, *Acanthina punctulata* (Sowerby), 25 mm (1"). It is very similar to the Angular Unicorn, but the spiral lines are more broken up, giving the shell a spotted appearance. It mostly lives on rocks of the upper intertidal. Monterey is the northern limit of its range.

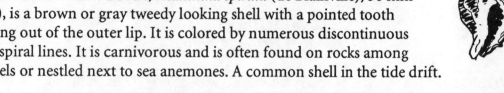

Spotted Unicorn

DOVE SHELLS
Family Columbellidae

The largest of the family is the COLUMBIA AMPHISSA, *Amphissa columbiana* Dall, 20 mm (¾"). It is gray or tan with a lavender cast to it, spotted with light brown. It lives under low intertidal and subtidal rocks. It is not common here.

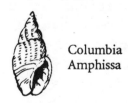

Columbia Amphissa

JOSEPH'S COAT, *Amphissa versicolor* Dall, 12 mm (½"), is smaller and prettier and much more common than its cousin, the Columbia Amphissa. It may be pale yellow, orange, brown, or gray and is sometimes spotted or dappled with brown. It also lives underneath rocks.

Jopseph's Coat

The smallest of the family here are the Mitrellas, not uncommon in fine tide drift. We seem to have three species, each so variable they blend into each other. In fact, a friend, knowledgeable in shells, thinks they are all members of the *M. carinata* complex.

However, I classify the plump ones with prominent rounded shoulders as KEELED DOVES, *Mitrella carinata* Hinds, 10 mm (⅜"), shiny, tannish or orange with dark tips. They often have broken lines around the whorls, or may be mottled. They live at the roots of eelgrass. Some recent reference books list this species under the genus *Alia*.

Keeled Dove

The LITTLE SPOTTED DOVE, *Mitrella gausapata* (Gould), 10 mm (⅜"), is cream or gray or tan, mottled with brown. The sides rise evenly toward the tip—there is no little bulged shoulder like on *Mitrella carinata*.

Little Spotted Dove

The slender very shiny ones are *Mitrella tuberosa* (Carpenter), 6 mm (¼"). It is apricot, tan, or cream, sometimes mottled, often with a lavender tinged tip.

Mitrella tuberosa

If these three tiny species of shells are too confusing, just label them SPOTTED DOVES, *Mitrella* species, and you won't be sticking your neck out in making possibly wrong identifications as I do.

DOG WHELKS
Family Nassariidae

The DOG WHELKS, or NASSAS, are carnivorous snails with strong shells. Reference books are not in agreement about descriptions of the various species, so my identifications were made by comparing them with the Stanford Geology Department collection. We seem to have five species here.

The smaller species are easily confused with the genus *Ocenebra*, but they can be identified by their anterior canals (between the inner lip and the shell's opening). In *Ocenebra* the anterior canal is thin and in *Nassarius* it is a wide notch.

Ocenebra   Nassarius

One of our very handsomest shells is the CHANNELED DOG WHELK, *Nassarius fossatus* (Gould), 45 mm (1¾"). The shiny outside of the shell is apricot, usually mixed with light gray or tan. The shells must be more fragile than they look, because they are usually broken when found in the tide drift. However, a perfect specimen is found often enough to keep us happy. No other shell has the striking orange parietal shield (to the left of the opening) which makes even fragments of shell easy to identify. They live under the surface of the sand at low tide and offshore.

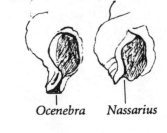
Channeled Dog Whelk

The CHECKED DOG WHELK, *Nassarius rhinetes* Berry, 35 mm (1⅜"), is tan or gray. The pronounced radial and axial (around and up and down) ribs cross to make a checkered pattern particularly effective in the gray phase when the sutures and the squares left between the ribs are white. It lives in deeper water, offshore, but commonly washes ashore near Waddell Creek.

Checked Dog Whelk

The FAT DOG WHELK, *Nassarius perpinguis* (Hinds), 25 mm (1"), is a nice little snail which should not have such a dreadful name, especially as it is apt to be slimmer than its checked cousin. The many axial and radial lines make a fine network pattern instead of the coarser checks of the Checked Dog Whelk. They live under the surface sand in middle and low tides. Like the Checked Dog Whelk, it is shades of tan or gray.

Fat Dog Whelk

The LEAN DOG WHELK, *Nassarius mendicus* (Gould), 13 mm (½"), is the least common and most inconspicuous of our nassas. It is smallest of them and most easily confused with *Ocenebra*. It is light and dark tan, often banded.

Lean
Dog Whelk

COOPER'S DOG WHELK, *Nassarius mendicus cooperi* (Forbes), 20 mm (¾"), is a rather handsome little shell, stouter than the Lean Dog Whelk; its fewer and more pronounced ribs make bumps on the whorls. Easily confused with a small *Ocenebra sclera* or *O. circumtexta*, it can be distinguished by the shape of its canal and also because it does not have the rough raspy feeling of *Ocenebra*. It is white with tan or brown lines around it.

Cooper's
Dog Whelk

MARGINELLAS
Family Marginellidae

The RICE SHELL, *Cystiscus jewettii* (Carpenter), 5 mm (¼'), is well-named. A pure white shiny shell the size of a rice grain, close examination shows that it is cone-shaped. It is rare here, found by sifting tidepool sand.

Rice Shell

Granula subtrigona (Carpenter), 3.5 mm (⅛"), looks very much like *C. jewettii*, but is slightly smaller and has tiny denticles inside the outer lip.

Granula subtrigona

Granulina margaritula (Carpenter), 3 mm (⅛"), is also white and closely resembles the above. It has a denticulate lip like *Granula*, but the aperture curves up over the spire.

Granulina margaritula

OLIVE SHELLS
Family Olividae

I don't know why the PURPLE DWARF OLIVE, *Olivella biplicata* (Sowerby) is called "dwarf." It is a good-sized, solid shell, highly polished, usually 20 mm (¾"). They live in colonies just under the sand at low, low tide. They are a very pretty beach shell.

Purple
Dwarf Olive

Looking at a day's find of these, it is hard to believe that shells of such varying sizes, shapes and colors are all the same species—big (1¼"), little (¼"), fat, thin, white, black, brown, tan, gray, mauve, plain and striped. It's no wonder the Indians used them for necklaces and traded them from tribe to tribe. Purple Olives have been found in Indian graves from coast to coast. Because they live only in the Pacific their occurrence has been useful in tracing the old Indian trade routes.

Nine out of ten of the beach shells found will have the tip of their spires worn off, which makes them easy to thread into a necklace—very pretty in their soft colors. But, alas, the colors fade, and eventually they are all a chalky gray, as are all those that lie in museum cases as examples of primitive Indian jewelry.

The SAN PEDRO OLIVE, *Olivella pycna* Berry, up to 10 mm (⅜"), looks like a baby Purple Dwarf Olive but is distinguished from these by being more slender and streaked with wavy lavender-brown lines. They are a very common beach shell found in fine gravel. *Olivella pedroana* Conrad is the same.

San Pedro
Olive

MITERS
Family Mitridae

Our representative of the family is IDA'S MITER, *Mitra idae* Melville, 65 mm (2½"), a solid shell, usually dark chocolate brown, but also found in light tan to almost black. In reference books it is always described as light brown, so perhaps ours is a sub-species. It lives in deep water, but is not uncommon in tide drift.

Ida's
Miter

NUTMEG SHELLS
Family Cancellariidae

A rare and handsome shell which would be a prize exhibit in any collection is the COOPER'S NUTMEG, *Cancellaria cooperi* Gabb, 75 mm (3"). It is yellowish with a lot of narrow reddish brown lines around it. I've only found bits and pieces in the tide drift of our beaches. Specimens are usually dredged up from deep water. It is a vegetarian. Malacologists haven't yet discovered what they feed on. Their teeth (radula) are strangely constructed.

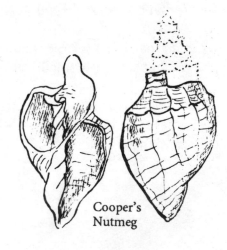

Cooper's
Nutmeg

CRAWFORD'S NUTMEG, *Cancellaria crawfordiana* Dall, 25 mm (1"). A yellow-tan and white shell with a white aperture, it is said to be rare. On outer coast beaches it is uncommon but not rare. It looks so much like the Checked Dog Whelk that for years I thought they were the same shell, although the very different shape of the canal was staring me in the face.

Crawford's Nutmeg

CONE SHELLS
Family Conidae

Cones are among the aristocrats of shelldom. The family contains some of the rarest and most beautiful shells to be found anywhere, but our one species is a rather insignificant member of the family.

The CALIFORNIA CONE, *Conus californicus* Hinds, 25 mm (1"), is small, tea-colored, sometimes with a hint of a purplish band around it. Like all cones, ours has a poisonous dart proboscis, but I never heard of anyone being hurt by it. The sting of some cones is fatal. They use the poison to paralyze the various snails, worms or fish they eat.

California Cone

TOWER SHELLS
Family Turridae

Towers are a large family, but only a few species are common here in beach drift. They are slender high-spired shells with a notch in posterior part (the part closer to tip of the spire) of the lip.

The YELLOW TOWER, *Megasurcula carpenteriana* (Gabb), 75 mm (3"), is a very large tower shell with cream-colored whorls and henna sutures. It is also called Carpenter's Tower. You won't find it in most reference books. I had to go to Stanford for its identification. One often finds recognizable pieces washed ashore, but a whole one is a great rarity.

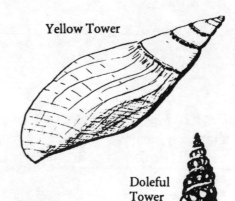

Yellow Tower

Doleful Tower

The DOLEFUL TOWER, *Pseudomelatoma torosa* (Carpenter), 20 mm (¾"), is a silly name for a little purple, brown, lumpy tower. It looks like a tough solid shell, but one practically never finds a whole one. It is washed ashore from deep water.

Incised Tower

INCISED TOWER, *Ophiodermella incisa* (Carpenter), 25 mm (1"). Another deep-water tower, sometimes washed ashore. It is pale tan or gray with reddish lines around the whorls.

Several very small turrids also can be found occasionally in beach drift. One of these, *Mitromorpha carpenteri* Gilbert, 6 mm (¼"), is brown with raised spiral cords.

Mitromorpha carpenteri

SMALL BUBBLE SHELLS
Family Acteonidae

The STRIPED BARREL SHELL, *Rictaxis punctocaelatus* (Carpenter), 10 mm (⅜"), is a handsome, very distictive little shell, rather uncommon here. It is pure white with two spiral bands of gray and numerous spiral grooves. Several have been found washed up on the beach near Soquel Point. Older books list it as *Acteon punctocaelatus*.

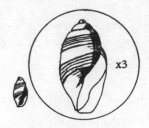

Striped Barrel Shell

GLASSY BUBBLE SHELLS
Family Scaphandridae

The BARREL BUBBLE, *Cylichnella culcitella* (Gould), 10 mm (⅜"), is bland in color but distinctive in shape. Fresh shells reportedly have a brown periostracum (a shellac-like coating on the shell exterior) with spiral lines. But the ones I've found are water worn and chalky white. It lives on the mudflats of bays or on soft bottoms offshore. It is listed in some reference books under the genus *Acteocina*.

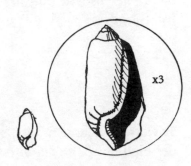

Barrel Bubble

PYRAMID SHELLS
Family Pyramidellidae

I don't know why these are called pyramid shells, for members of this family come in many shapes, none of which resembles a pyramid. They are all small shells, some short and fat, others tall and slender. They are apparently parasitic on other invertebrates.

Iselica ovoidea (Gould), 5 mm (¼"), is a small translucent white snail found in tidepool sand now and then. It is circled with sharp spiral grooves. It lives on the mantles of abalones.

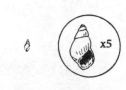

Iselica ovoidea

The tiny, white, almost translucent shell *Odostomia phanea* Dall and Bartsch, 2 mm (1/16"), needs a magnifying glass for appreciation. It is smooth and shiny and the large whorl is sort of bulbous. We find them in tidepool sand. Uncommon, but perhaps if we did more sand-sifting they'd turn out to be more common. They live on rocks or on abalone shells. A number of other species of *Odostomia* also occur in Monterey Bay.

Odostomia phanea

The *Turbonilla* snails, to 7 mm (5/16"), are the tall, slender members of the family. Some are white, others brown. All have numerous axial ribs on each whorl. If you have a good hand lens, examine the nuclear whorls at the tip of the spire. They spiral around an axis perpendicular to the later whorls. There are many species.

Turbonilla

MARSH SNAILS
Family Melampidae

The MARSH SNAIL, *Ovatella myosotis* (Draparnaud), 6 mm (¼"), is a thin, brown, transluscent shell. It lives mostly in marshes such as Elkhorn Slough, though it has also been found in beach drift near Capitola. This species is thought to have been introduced from Europe.

Marsh Snail

LAND SNAILS

When winter storms flood our local creeks, land snail shells are sometimes washed out to sea. Then the waves bring them back and leave them with the tide drift. There are three species, one introduced and two native, that I have found on local beaches. Dr. Katherine Palmer of the Paleontological Research Institution at Ithaca, New York, was kind enough to identify them for me.

The introduced snail, the GARDEN SNAIL, *Helix aspersa* Müller, to 40 mm (1½"), is the common snail pest in local gardens. It is often beautifully patterned, tan and brown stripes and splotches and zigzag designs.

G Dallas Hanna (see references) reported several sinistrally coiled (counter-clockwise) specimens from the gardens in the San Francisco Bay area. Such oddities are rare and worth watching for.

Garden Snail

This snail was introduced to California from Europe in the 1850s (partly for food and partly by accident) and has since spread widely across the western United States. I didn't see it at Rancho del Oso until after 1960—probably it came with imported garden plants. They taste a bit like abalone. The harvesting of them for food should be encouraged; it might keep them under control.

To prepare them for eating put them into a pail with salt and vinegar—stir and let stand 30 minutes. Rinse in running water until water is clear. Put in boiling salted water to cover for 30 minutes. When cool pull meat out of shell and cut off the dark portion. Rinse snails in warm water. Simmer until tender (2 hours) in water with wine, onion, salt. Put a little garlic butter in scrubbed shells, plug with garlic butter. Place those you want to cook (rest can be frozen and given to friends) in pie tin with a little wine in bottom. Bake 7 minutes at 475 degrees and serve.

The native WOOD SNAIL, *Haplotrema* sp., 20 mm (¾"), has a small flattish shell which varies from black through brown to white. All the live ones I have seen are tan, brown or black; perhaps the white shells are bleached-out ones. They live in damp places, under logs and stones.

Wood Snail

The REDWOOD SNAIL, *Helminthoglypta* cf. *H. nickliniana* (Lea), is very fragile, tan to brown, sometimes with a dark stripe around the sutures of the whorls. The largest one I've seen is 40 mm (1½"); usually they are about 20 mm (¾"). They live in forest duff.

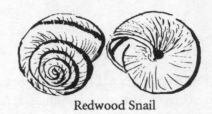

Redwood Snail

There are other land snail species native to this region, but as yet no handy guidebook has been written for identifying them. Some have a microsculpture—such as patterns of minute bumps—on the shell. These require a microscope to see.

PART TWO: CLASS PELECYPODA

These are the bivalves or clams and include cockles, oysters, piddocks, scallops, and mussels. They are arranged here as they are in most shell books, which means we must begin with two of the rarest kinds that wash up on our beaches.

NUT CLAMS
Family Nuculanidae

The GROOVED NUT, *Nuculana taphria* Dall, 20 mm (¾"), is a neat little clam, about the size and color of a blanched almond. It almost looks and feels like ivory. It is an offshore mollusk not commonly washed ashore—rare enough for me to say "thank you, waves" when I find one.

Grooved Nut

BITTERSWEET CLAMS
Family Glycymeridae

I suppose I should mention this little clam although I have found only one valve, and never another one. Because I found one, there are probably others around, so it must not be left out. It is the BITTERSWEET, *Glycymeris subobsoleta* Carpenter. The diameter of my specimen is 20 mm (¾") and the color yellowish-gray except where it is worn white. It reportedly lives offshore.

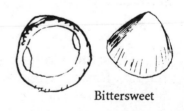

Bittersweet

MINUTE PENS
Family Phylobryidae

Phylobrya setosa

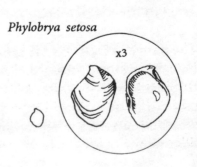

x3

The tiny *Phylobrya setosa* (Carpenter), length to 5 mm (¼"), resembles a minature mussel or pen shell. The ones I have found are cream or pinkish colored, with a pearly interior. I have found only a few, but they are so small they could easily be overlooked.

MUSSELS
Family Mytilidae

We have both species of the large edible mussels living on our rocks, both delicious but both poisonous during the warm summer months. The cause of the poison is the "red tide," produced by a microscopic planktonic organism called *Gonyaulax*. In the winter months the mussels are usually safe to eat. A New Year's Day picnic, with a big pot of sea water to drop in the mussels, French bread, red wine, and plenty of melted butter, is a rare treat. We just take the big ones, leaving room for the crowded little ones to grow. But, sadly, in many areas they are being stripped from our rocks by fishermen who scrape them off to find fishing worms underneath. Since one mussel lays several million eggs each year, it probably wouldn't take long for them to re-establish themselves if the fishermen could be persuaded to leave them alone.

Our most abundant mussel is the CALIFORNIA MUSSEL, *Mytilus californianus* Conrad. It is blue-black in color, sometimes with brown. It is oblong and commonly grows to 180 mm (7") but is usually less than half that size. Even larger ones sometimes wash up on the beach, ripped from wharf pilings during storms. The outside of the shell has deep lumpy growth rings, usually crossed by radial grooves. Inside, it is a shining midnight blue. They like to live on intertidal surf-swept rocks in close-packed communities, secured by tough threads called byssus. Sometimes one finds small pearls in them, white, pink, brown, or black.

California Mussel

The BLUE MUSSEL, *Mytilus edulis* Linnaeus, about 50 mm (2") long, is the usual edible mussel found in cold seas all over the world. It seems to prefer quieter waters than the California Mussel and is abundant in harbors. On the pier at Seacliff Beach, both species live together. It is rare on the outer coast, but a few shells have washed up north of Greyhound Rock. It is easily distinguished from the California Mussel by its wedge shape and the lack of radial ridges crossing the shallow growth lines.

Blue Mussel

The next group of mussels to be considered are the horse mussels (I don't know what they have to do with horses), genus *Modiolus*.

CARPENTER'S HORSE MUSSEL, *Modiolus carpenteri* Soot-Ryen, 30 mm (1¼"), is a small shell, exterior white, with a chestnut-brown periostracum and fuzzy bristles on the posterior end of the shell. Interior is whitish, sometimes with violet. It commonly washes up on some of our beaches from the subtidal. Listed in older works as *Modiolus fornicatus*.

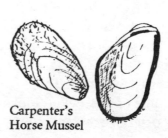

Carpenter's Horse Mussel

The STRAIGHT HORSE MUSSEL, *Modiolus rectus* (Conrad), reaches a length of 130 mm (5"). Fresh specimens are covered with a beautiful yellowish-brown periostracum. It is an attractive shell, but prone to cracking when it dries. It only ocassionally washes up on beaches of the outer coast. It lives offshore. Large ones with a twist in the shell used to be called *Modiolus flabellatus*, but are the same species.

Straight Horse Mussel

The third group of mussels are the rock-boring mussels, of which there are two genera. All are long, slender, fragile shells with a shiny, dark brown periostracum and a pearly blue-white interior. In a collection, the periostracum will dry and flake off unless oiled.

The CALIFORNIA PEA POD, *Adula californiensis* (Philipi), 25 mm (1"), is a very fragile, narrow, shiny dark brown shell except where the periostracum is worn off near the beaks, showing bluish white. The beak is near the posterior (fatter) end, which is covered with fine bristly stubble. It bores into clay and soft rock.

California Pea Pod

The FALCATE DATE, *Adula falcata* (Gould), is similar to the Pea Pod but twice as big, sometimes 75 mm (3") long. It is not quite as fragile, and the periostracum is much more wrinkled. The inside is white. It bores into shale and is not uncommon near Capitola.

Falcate Date

The ROCK BORER, *Lithophaga plumula* (Hanley), 25 mm (1"), is aptly named. *Lithophaga* literaly means "rock eater." Of course it doesn't actually eat rock, but bores into the rock for protection. I find it amazing that these delicate shells can drill into hard stone. They reportedly secrete an acid which dissolves some of the rock. It looks similar to the others, but the posterior end tapers.

Rock Borer

OYSTERS
Family Ostreidae

The NATIVE OYSTER, *Ostrea lurida* Carpenter, 50 mm (2"), is the only oyster native to this region. The shell exterior is a mottled gray, sometimes with pink, scaly in texture; interior greenish. They are said to be quite tasty, but are rather small. They live attached to rocks and pilings intertidally in Elkhorn Slough and in calmer parts of Monterey Bay.

Native Oyster

The JAPANESE OYSTER, *Crassostrea gigas* (Thunberg), 200 mm (8"), has at various times been introduced to this region, particularly at Elkhorn Slough. It comes in a variety of shapes, gray outside and white inside. In the late 1960s and early '70s I found several Japanese Oysters washed up on the beach near Waddell Creek. The shellfish farm at Pigeon Point was experimenting with several oyster species including *C. gigas*. I suppose that various colonies of non-indigenous species may have formed from escaped eggs or spat.

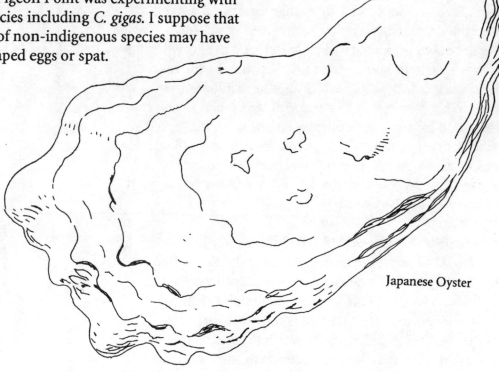

Japanese Oyster

SCALLOPS
Family Pectinidae

Perhaps no other shape in nature has been used so extensively as an art motif than that of the scallop. It was used, not only as a practical design as in pre-Grecian pottery, but as decoration on Grecian vases. It has also been a part of religious mystique in many lands. Aphrodite was born from a scallop shell, crusaders used scallops on their coats-of-arms to show they had been to Palestine, a holy radiance seems to shine from scallops in Renaissance paintings, in sculpture it has been carved in stone for palaces and cathedrals, Venetian glass makers incorporated it in their incomparable work, jewel craftsmen fashioned it in gold and silver, and the French weavers wove it into tapestry.

There is no match for the beauty of its subtle simple symmetry. It seems to hold an irresistible charm; children may pass other shells by in the sand, but they almost always pick up bright beautiful scallops with delight.

We have three scallops on our beach, the GIANT ROCK SCALLOP, *Hinnites giganteus* Gray, is one of the most common shells in the sand, although one can no longer find live shells on the rocks at low tide as we used to. It is hunted as a "rock oyster" and, because it is very slow growing, the population all along our coast has been greatly depleted.

The Giant Rock Scallop starts life as a classic scallop, swimming around like other scallops, flapping its shells like a butterfly. In this stage it is a pretty little shell, 25 mm (1") or less across, colored usually orange inside and out, but sometimes pure white, yellow, or marked with brown. Then it settles down on a rock like an oyster, and the growth rings become rough and lumpy and misshapen to fit the rock. The outside is brown and white and the inside is shiny white. Whatever its color or shape or size, it can always be recognized by a magenta purple stain near the hinge. No other scallop species has this purple stain, and the Giant Rock Scallops always have it. The largest of these shells I have ever found was 180 mm (7") across. Older books list it as *Hinnites multirugosus*.

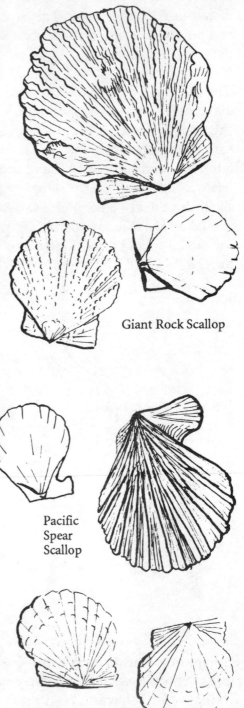

Giant Rock Scallop

Pacific Spear Scallop

Broad-winged Scallop

The PACIFIC SPEAR SCALLOP, *Chlamys hastata* (Sowerby), 40 mm (1½"), is a handsome shell not often found here. It lives in deep water. It is shaped very much like a young Giant Rock Scallop but taller. It can be distinguished by the fact that is has much stronger ribs, sometimes in pairs, and between these deep ribs are weak beaded ribs. It usually comes in shades of yellow or pink.

Our third scallop, found only occasionally, is the BROAD-WINGED SCALLOP, *Leptopecten latiauratus* Conrad, 25 mm (1") wide. It is usually brown with white zigzags, but I've found orange ones. It has a characteristically lopsided look because its ears are set at an oblique angle. It is free-swimming and lives in shallow water around rocks, sand, and seaweed.

FILE SHELLS
Family Limidae

The FILE SHELL, *Limaria hemphilli* (Hertlein & Strong), 24 mm (¹⁵⁄₁₆"), is white with very fine radiating ribs. It resembles a scallop, but is asymmetrical and has smaller "ears." It washes up only rarely in Monterey Bay, this being the northern limit of its range. Listed in older references as *Lima hemphilli*.

File Shell

JINGLE SHELLS
Family Anomiidae

Our Jingle Shell, or PEARLY MONIA, *Pododesmus cepio* (Gray), 50 mm (2"), is irresistibly lovely: it is hard to come home from the beach without a pocketful of these sea-green and lavender irridescent shells. When I get enough I string and hang them for wind chimes. They measure up to 75 mm (3") wide, but are usually about 50 mm. The lower valve, often pearly white, has a hole in the middle where it joins the rock or whatever it is attached to. The outside of the upper valve is brown or greenish and sometimes symmetrical and very pretty. It is broad minded in its choice of homes and is found on kelp stands, on piers, and often on large Red Abalone shells. It is an edible "rock oyster."

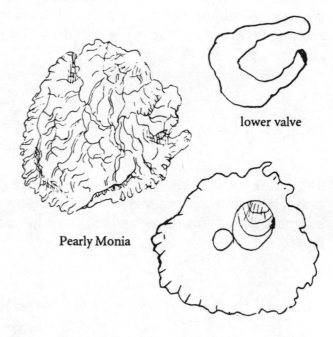

lower valve

Pearly Monia

The AMBER JINGLE, *Anomia peruviana* d'Orbigny, 50 mm (2"), is extremely rare here, being more common to the south. It is an exquisite, waxy, opalescent, peach color. The shell is much thinner than the Pearly Monia and has three instead of two muscle scars.

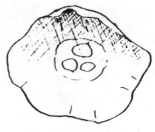

Amber Jingle

CARDITAS
Family Carditidae

CARPENTER'S CARDITA, *Glans subquadrata* (Carpenter), 6-12 mm (¼"-½"), is a pretty little cockle-like shell, tough and distinctive. It has strong ribs radiating from small beaks. The outside is spotted and streaked light and dark brown and white, inside is white. It lives under stones in shallow water. We find them decorating the sea anemones or lying in tidepool sand.

Carpenter's Cardita

JEWEL BOXES
Family Chamidae

On our beaches I have found only one species of jewel box clam, the AGATE JEWEL BOX, *Chama arcana* Bernard, 40 mm (1½"). This usually insignificant but occasionally handsome shell looks like inexpensive china stained haphazardly with bright pink rays. They are white marked with pink. It is roughly cup-shaped, but adapts its shape to its environment. Under a magnifying glass the margins are minutely toothed. It is not uncommon locally. Handsome specimens have pink and orange frills on the outside. It lives attached to rocks and is an edible "rock oyster." Older works list it as *Chama pellucida* Broderip.

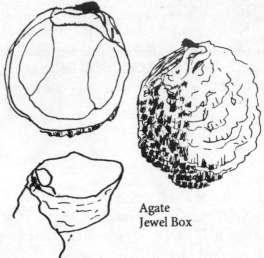

Agate Jewel Box

LUCINES
Family Lucinidae

The CALIFORNIA LUCINE, *Epilucina californica* (Conrad), 35 mm (1⅜"), is white, has a narrow, dainty hinge, a concentric sculpture of very fine ridges, and has no periostracum. It lives in gravel.

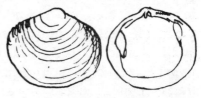

California Lucine

DIPLODONS
Family Ungulinidae

The PACIFIC ORB DIPLODON, *Diplodonta orbella* (Gould), to 20 mm (¾"), is similar to the lucine, but more inflated. The shell is white, smooth except for growth lines, with a brown periostracum (usually worn off in tide-drift shells). It lives in gravel and under rocks, intertidally and subtidally.

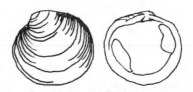

Pacific Orb Diplodon

LEPTONS
Families Erycinidae and Kelliidae

The LITTLE BOX LEPTON, *Lasaea subviridis* Dall, family Erycinidae, is a tiny 2 mm (¹⁄₁₆") magenta-bordered, pinkish, obese, transparent shell. It lives among mussels; empty shells occur on sea anemones. Some authors recognize a second, very similar species, *Lasaea cistula* Keen, living in the same habitat.

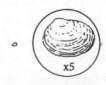

x5

Little Box Lepton

The KELLY SHELL, *Kellia laperousii* (Deshayes), family Kelliidae, 25 mm (1"), is fat, almost balloonish, and usually has traces of its shiny yellowish-brown periostracum. It can be distinguished from other bivalves by the wide gap in the hinge line. It lives among mussels.

Kelly Shell

Family Corbiculidae

I have found several JAPANESE CLAMS, *Corbicula manilensis* (Philipi), 35 mm (1⅜"), on our beaches. They have a thick, triangular shell with concentric ridges, blackish brown on the outside, purple and white inside. They are freshwater clams and I don't know what they are doing on the beach. In the San Joaquin Valley they are so abundant that they clog pipelines. Perhaps the shells on our beach are from fishermen's bait boxes.

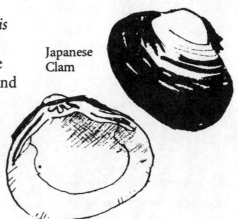

Japanese Clam

VENUS CLAMS
Family Veneridae

Members of this large family are mostly white. I don't suppose one has to be an absolute nut about shells to be enthusiastic about white clams, but it probably helps. Be that as it may, I find their subtle shades of whiteness, their graceful profiles and changing shadows of matchless beauty, best described by the Japanese concept "shibui"—understated exquisite perfection.

Few people stop to pick up a plain white clam shell. For that reason, no matter how many people are on the beach, I'll still find shells—sometimes perfect specimens—to add to our collection.

The beaches near where I lived for many years, at Waddell Creek, were not "clamming" beaches. We didn't have people with spades and rakes ploughing up the sand and getting themselves drowned in the potholes and undertow as they do at Moss Landing. Because storms washed away our sand nearly every winter (and brought it back in the spring) the habitat was not stable enough to support a large population of burrowing clams. Nevertheless, in sheltered areas around the rocky points a few clams would find homes and their shells wash up along the tide drift to delight me with their beauty.

It would be impossible to take a walk along our beach without finding at least broken pieces of the PACIFIC LITTLENECK, *Protothaca staminea* (Conrad), 40 mm (1½"). Usually it is a chalky roundish white shell. However, often it has designs in henna or yellow-brown very much like the designs on Indian baskets. I think the Indians must have found the inspiration for their patterns here. It lives among gravel and under rocks.

Pacific Littleneck

A variety of the Pacific Littleneck is sometimes listed in shell books as *Prototheca staminea ruderata* (Deshayes). It is white, sometimes with brown staining, and has concentric lamellae (frills around it). Both these clams live shallowly in the sand between loose rocks.

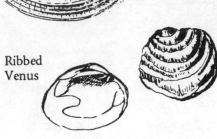

Prototheca staminea ruderata

A clam very similar to the frilled variety of the Pacific Littleneck is the RIBBED VENUS, *Irus lamellifer* (Conrad), 20 mm (¾"). It is white, with prominent concentric frills, and often a rather squashed look, perhaps because it squeezes into rock crevices. The Ribbed Venus lacks the fine radiating ridges of the Pacific Littleneck.

Ribbed Venus

The THIN-SHELLED LITTLENECK, *Prototheca tenerrima* (Carpenter), 100 mm (4"), is sculptured by a combination of fine radiating ridges with thicker concentric ridges. Close examination of the sculpture will distinguish it from the Washington Clam (below), which lacks the radiating sculpture. It is also less inflated, with a thinner shell. It lives in Elkhorn Slough, and also sometimes washes up on beaches from offshore.

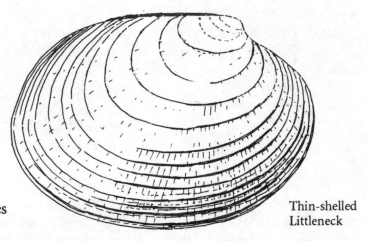

Thin-shelled Littleneck

The WASHINGTON CLAM, *Saxidomus nuttalli* Conrad, grows to 130 mm (5"). It has a large toothed hinge, and pieces of dried ligament are apt to be attached to the beach shells. It burrows in the sand of bays and in rocky intertidal areas along the coast. Specimens from rocky areas are apt to be rounder and chunkier with a smoother sculpture. Beach shells are white stained with yellow.

Washington Clam

The QUAHOG, *Mercenaria mercenaria* (Linnaeus),
60 mm (2⅜"), (pronounced kō´-hog) is a thick-shelled
clam with raised concentric growth ridges. Shell is
white, sometimes with an orangey tinge; inside white
with some purple. This clam is native to the Atlantic
Coast where it is widely harvested for food. It has been
introduced in several California bays and is often
imported by restaurants. Perry collected several from
the beach at Capitola in 1980; perhaps they "escaped"
from someone's dinner.

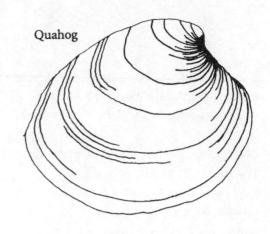

Quahog

The JAPANESE LITTLENECK, *Tapes japonica*
Deshayes, 60 mm (2⅜"), is another non-native bivalve.
It is thought to have been accidentally introduced with
Japanese Oysters. It closely resembles the Pacific Little-
neck, but is more elongate, with purple on the interior.
Empty shells can be found on the mudflats at Elkhorn
Slough.

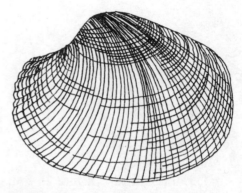

Japanese Littleneck

Perhaps the most famous of our
clams is the PISMO CLAM, *Tivela
stultorum* (Mawe). It is easily recognized by its triangular shape and very
thick shell. It grows to about 125 mm
(5"), but large ones are rare now.
Small ones, about 2 inches, are not
uncommon on the beach at Seacliff
and Rio del Mar. At various times in
the past, large clams were abundant
here, and at low tide clammers would
rake them up by the dozen. In the
old days some people even used
plows to get them. The Pismo population was so decimated that, like the
sardine, it has yet to recover. Sea
otters also eat them.

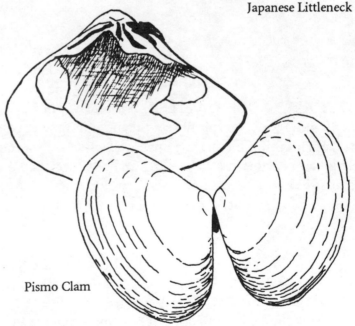

Pismo Clam

One of the smallest of the venus clams is the GEM CLAM, *Gemma
gemma* (Totten), 5 mm (¼"). This tiny clam is abundant in parts of
Elkhorn Slough, but easily overlooked because of its small size. It is
white, roughly triangular in shape, with fine concentric ridges and
a purple spot near the beak. It was introduced from the East Coast,
probably with oysters.

Gem Clam

51

COCKLES
Family Cardiidae

Two species of cockles are found here. Both are yellowish white. They burrow shallowly in sand at the lowest tide level and offshore. Although clams in other families are sometimes called "cockles," the name is best reserved for this family to avoid confusion.

NUTTALL'S COCKLE, *Clinocardium nuttallii*
(Conrad), is about 75 mm (3")
and has up to 37 square
ribs crossed by wavy
lines.

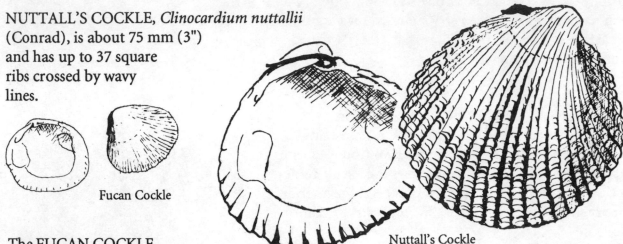

Fucan Cockle

Nuttall's Cockle

The FUCAN COCKLE,
Clinocardium fucanum Dall,
is smaller and rounder, about 25 mm (1") wide, but it has more ribs—forty or more.

ROCK DWELLERS
Family Petricolidae

The HEART ROCK-DWELLER, *Petricola carditoides* (Conrad), to 40 mm (1½"), is typically round and plump with concentric ridges and minute radiating lines; dull white with some brown. This clam nestles in rock crevices and old bore-clam holes. It comes in many shapes and sizes, depending on the shape of the hole in which it lived. It can also bore.

Heart Rock-dweller

DISH AND SURF CLAMS
Family Mactridae

One of the most conspicuous of our white clams is the large PACIFIC GAPER, *Tresus nuttallii* (Conrad). It grows to be six or more inches (150 mm) and is quite common, particularly south of Año Nuevo Point. It is also common in Elkhorn Slough where it is lives a foot or two deep in the mud. Empty shells are often discarded by clammers. The Gaper has a characteristic cuplike hinge (chondrophore) on both valves, a brown periostracum, and a large gape between the valves where the siphon is located. Small two-inch-long oval individuals sometimes wash in from intertidal reefs. Perhaps they adopt this shape from nestling among rocks. Even small specimens are easily identified by the hinge shape.

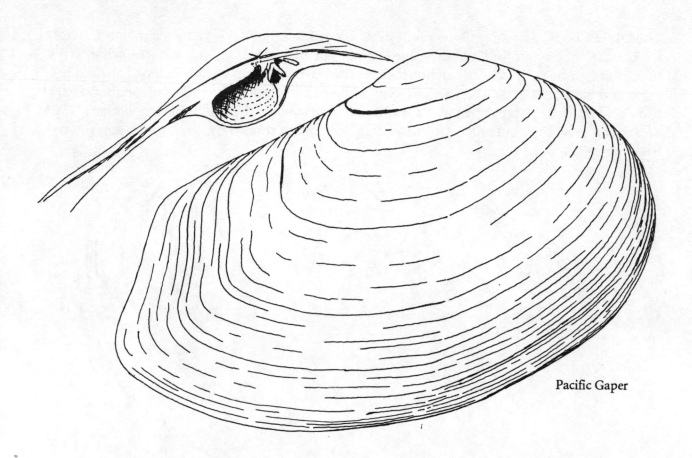

Pacific Gaper

Tresus capax (Gould), 180 mm (7"), is a close
relative of the Pacific Gaper, somewhat
triangular in outline. It is a more
northern species, rare in
Monterey Bay.

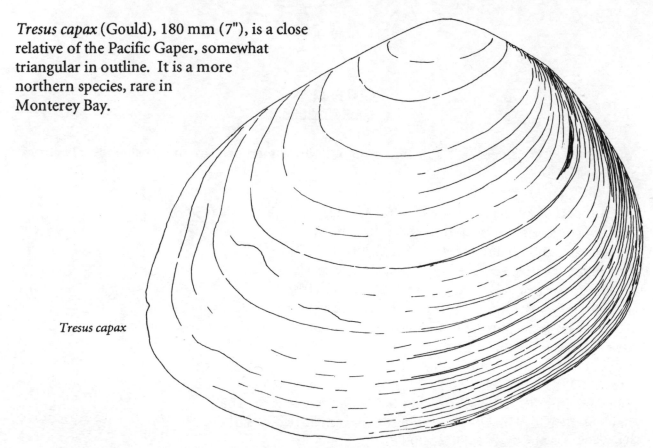

Tresus capax

The DISH CLAM, *Spisula catilliformis* Conrad, about 130 mm (5"), is just a plain, nondescript, white clam. You won't find it in most shell books. The hinge has a chondrophore similar to that of *Tresus*, but the shell lacks the siphonal gape. The valves are thin, usually chipped around the edge, and don't fit together very well. It lives offshore, but commonly washes up on the beach at Rio del Mar. There, large storm waves washed up thousands of this species in late January, 1981. The clams were dead, but with soft parts intact. After about three days, the waves swept them back out to sea.

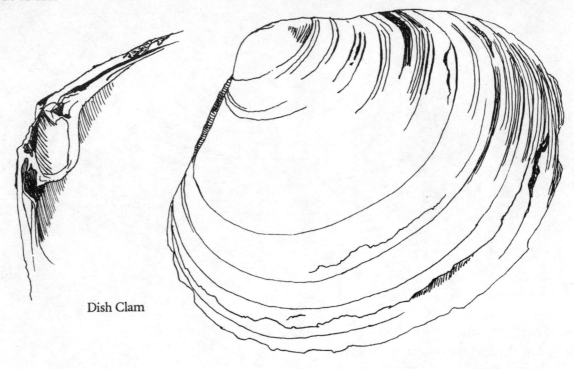

Dish Clam

TELLINS
Family Tellinidae

And now we'll consider the Tellin family, among whose members are the most gracefully curved of clam shells.

The princess of our tellins is the BODEGA TELLIN, *Tellina bodegensis* Hinds, 60 mm (2⅜"). It is shiny, translucent, smooth and highly polished, looking as though it were made of fine bone china. It is pure white except for an apricot wash inside the valves. This clam is evidently a favorite food of some shell-boring creature because a large proportion of the shells I have found have a neat round hole drilled in them.

Bodega Tellin

The MODEST TELLIN, *Tellina modesta* (Carpenter), 20 mm (¾"), is a small, smooth, shiny white clam with a thin fragile shell. The shape of the pallial line best distinguishes it from its relatives. It lives offshore but sometimes washes in.

Modest Tellin

Also in this family are the Macomas, flat white clams with graceful, slightly twisted posteriors. The BENT-NOSE MACOMA (as a child I refused to accept such an ugly name for such a graceful shell—I called it the "Smiling Clam"), *Macoma nasuta* (Conrad), to 65 mm (2½"), occasionally washes up on our beaches and is abundant in Elkhorn Slough.

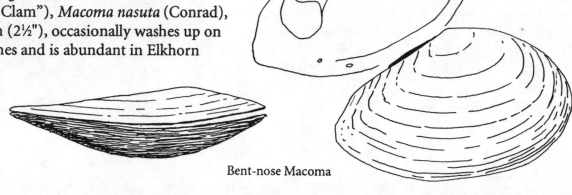

Bent-nose Macoma

Its close relative, the IRUS MACOMA, *Macoma inquinata* (Deshayes), 35 mm (1⅜"), has only a very slight twist to the shell. Its creamy-white shell is more inflated than the Bent-nose. Some books list it as *Macoma irus*.

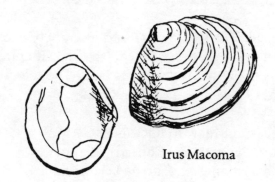

Irus Macoma

The largest of our Macomas is the WHITE MACOMA, *Macoma secta* (Conrad), to 90 mm (3 ½"). It is smooth, shiny, pure white, thin-shelled, with a thin periostracum. There is a thin blade-like protruberence of the shell between the ligament and posterior end. Common in Elkhorn Slough.

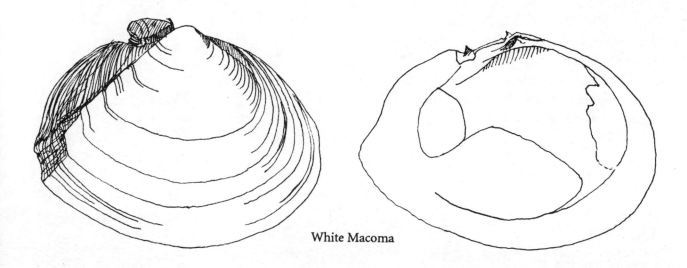

White Macoma

Finally, there is the INDENTED MACOMA, *Macoma indentata* Carpenter, 40 mm (1½"). It is usually small, shiny and fragile; often elongated with a rather pointed posterior end. It lives just offshore buried in sand. Sometimes during storms larger specimens are ripped up by the waves and cast upon our beaches. An exceptionally large (74 mm) specimen was collected from the beach at Rio del Mar in 1981 and is now in the collection of the California Academy of Sciences.

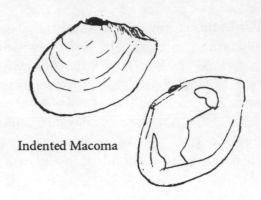

Indented Macoma

SANGUIN CLAMS
Family Psammobiidae

Three species from this family occur in Monterey Bay. In a gross sense, they don't much resemble each other. But they have been grouped into the same family because of similarities in the shape of the hinge teeth, position of the ligament, and other features.

The SUNSET CLAM, *Gari californica* (Conrad), is oval in shape, thin-shelled, whitish, with pinkish rays radiating out from the beak. The coloration is said to resemble a sunset. Rare.

The beautiful MAHOGANY CLAM, *Nuttallia nuttallii* (Conrad), 75 mm (3"), is a smooth, flattened clam with a shiny mahogany-colored periostracum. Interior purplish, valves unequally inflated. Occasional in Elkhorn Slough. Listed in older books as *Sanguinolaria nuttallii*.

The JACKKNIFE CLAM, *Tagelus californianus* (Conrad), 75 mm (3"), is elongated with a brown periostracum. It resembles the razor clams (below) but is more inflated and the periostracum is dull rather than shiny.

Sunset Clam

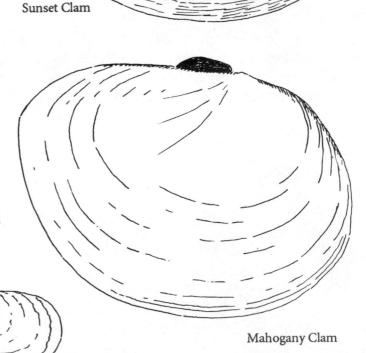

Mahogany Clam

Jackknife Clam

SEMELE CLAMS
Family Semelidae

The CALIFORNIA CUMINGIA, *Cumingia californica* Conrad, 30 mm (1¼"), could be called the masquerader of our mollusca. It is shaped like a macoma, is white, and even has the twist at the posterior end. Yet it belongs to an entirely separate family. Its true identity is revealed by its hinge, which has a spoon-shaped process or chondrophore something like the dish clams. The exterior has irregular concentric ridges.

California Cumingia

One of the scarcest of our bivalves is the ROCK-DWELLING SEMELE, *Semele rupicola* Dall, 40 mm (1½"). It is roughly oval in outline, moderately inflated, white, with small irregular concentric ridges. A lovely pink rims the interior.

RAZOR CLAMS
Family Solenidae

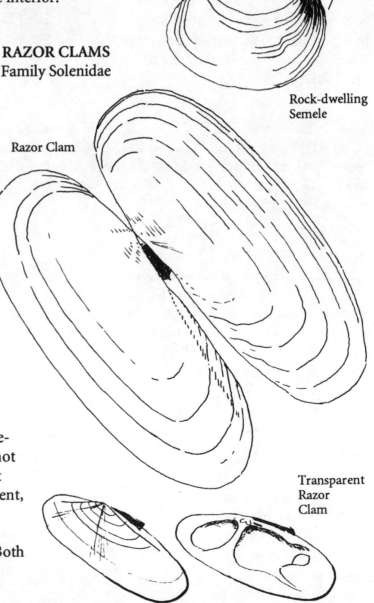

Rock-dwelling Semele

Razor Clam

Transparent Razor Clam

I occasionally find the shells of RAZOR CLAMS, family Solenidae. These are fragile and lovely, but I rarely find a beach shell whole. We have two species. The large one, *Siliqua patula* (Dixon), grows to about 150 mm (6"), but I've not found it larger than 100 mm (4"). It is smooth, shiny yellow-brown except where the periostracum is worn off, and there it is ringed with cream and lavender. Inside it is white, tinted with cream and lavender. A strong white rib extends from the beak across the interior.

The TRANSPARENT RAZOR CLAM, *Siliqua lucida* (Conrad), has the same description as the big Razor Clam, but is not more than 45 mm (2") and is somewhat slimmer in outline. The shell is tranluscent, showing the lovely rays of lavender and brown through to the interior, and also through the shiny skin on the outside. Both species are sand dwellers and very fast diggers.

SOFT-SHELL CLAMS
Family Myidae

A chalky, inflated, medium-sized clam that might, at first glance, be confused with a Gaper is the CHUBBY MYA, *Platyodon cancellatus* (Conrad), 100 mm (4"). It has a spoonlike hinge (chondrophore) on the left valve which sticks out at right angles, and the right valve has a hollow to fit it. The difference between it and the Gaper is that the Gaper's cups are on both valves and lie horizontal with the rest of the shell. The Chubby Mya bores into the soft shale common along the coast at Santa Cruz. It is white with fine concentric ridges.

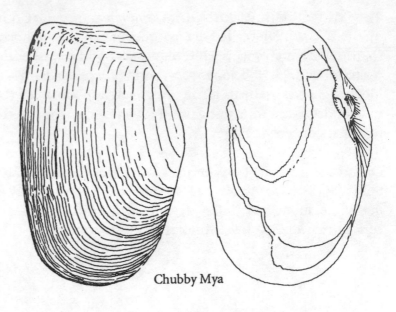

Chubby Mya

The CALIFORNIA SOFT-SHELL CLAM, *Cryptomya californica* (Conrad), 25 mm (1"), is a rather dull, nondescript little clam. It is white, oval, and rather flattened. The hinge is shaped like that of the Chubby Mya. It lives intertidally on the mudflats of Elkhorn Slough and offshore in sand.

California Soft-shell Clam

Another SOFT-SHELL CLAM, *Mya arenaria* Linnaeus, 75 mm (3"), is smooth, oval in outline, with a very thin periostracum. The valves gape (don't fit together very well), and it has the same characteristic hinge. This is an introduced species which now lives in Elkhorn Slough. Fishermen sometimes use them for bait, discarding the shells in places where the clams do not live, such as along the San Lorenzo River.

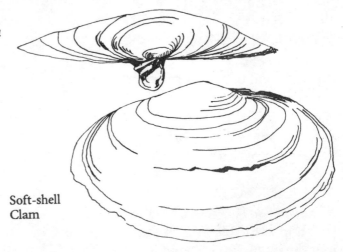

Soft-shell Clam

A tiny and uncommon shell belonging to the same family is the FRAGILE SPHENIA, *Sphenia fragilis* Carpenter. It is about 15 mm (½") long with a round bulbous body and a twisted snout. It will take a magnifying glass to see that the left valve has a chondrophore (sticking out tooth) and the right valve a socket for it to fit in. It is chalky white.

Fragile Sphenia

SAXICAVES
Family Hiatellidae

The ARCTIC ROCK BORER, *Hiatella arctica* (Linnaeus), 35 mm (1⅜"), is native to both the north Pacific and north Atlantic. It is not a very pretty clam: chalky white, irregular in shape, with a dull brown skin that has partly peeled off. The pallial line is not a line at all, but a series of discontinous scars. It nestles in crevices and bores into rocks. *Hiatella pholadis* (Linnaeus) may be the same species.

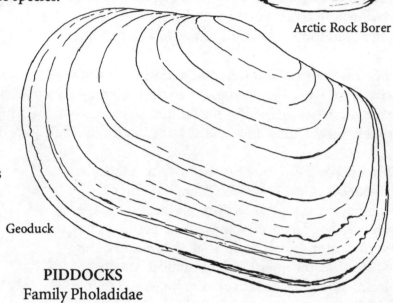

Arctic Rock Borer

I mention the GEODUCK (pronounced gooey-duck), *Panopea generosa* (Gould), 125 mm (5"), because it is known to occur in Elkhorn Slough and offshore. It is a very deep burrower, however, and neither the author nor editor have ever found an empty shell here. It is common as a fossil in Pliocene deposits near Capitola.

Geoduck

PIDDOCKS
Family Pholadidae

These clams are all white with rough ridges on the anterior end of their shells. The clams use the rough edge of their shell in a grinding action to bore into hard substrates such as rock or other shells. All have a spoon-like projection on the interior of the shell.

We'll start with the smallest and easiest to identify of the piddocks, the ABALONE BORER, *Penitella conradi* Valenciennes, 5 mm (¼"). It is a common shell. If you find a small roundish piddock which has bored into a RED ABALONE shell, this is it. If you open a "black pearl" in the inside of an abalone you'll probably find an Abalone Borer in the middle; the abalone has built the pearl as protection. It also bores into mussels.

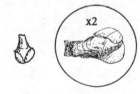

Abalone Borer

Identifying the other piddocks is frustrating because of varying sizes and shapes and confusing reference books. I gave up trying to identify ones I had found near Waddell Creek, and took my collection to Stanford for help from Myra Keen's students. I don't often do this because I think it is an imposition to take their time except as a last resort. When I'd climbed the three flights of iron stairs in the old Geology building and arrived at the shell collection on the top floor, I found that the students also had piddock problems; they had discovered a lot misidentified in the collection! If experts make mistakes, thought I, what hope for me? However, after consultation we decided the Waddell piddocks were of two species: *Penitella richardsoni* (formerly *Penitella gabbii*) and *Penitella penita*.

The stubby gaping one about 40 mm (1½") is *Penitella richardsoni* (Kennedy), and the long bulbous one, sometimes 80–100 mm (3 to 4"), is the FLAP-TIPPED PIDDOCK, *Penitella penita* (Conrad). You'll find them both washed ashore, or you can sometimes break them out of cobbles that wash up on the beach. It and some of the other piddocks are reportedly good eating, but taking them for food is no longer legal. How they make their holes in shale is a mystery to me. I'm told they do it by turning around and around, but their shells are far softer than some of the rock into which they bore.

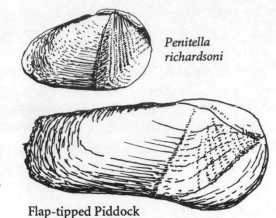

Penitella richardsoni

Flap-tipped Piddock

These and most of our other piddocks have a widely gaping anterior end while the animal is actively growing and boring. When the clam matures and ceases boring, it grows a smooth extension to its shell called the callum, which seals off the anterior end. Because of this, mature and immature individuals of the same species can look quite different to the untrained eye.

Other piddocks in the Monterey Bay area include the giant SCALE-SIDED PIDDOCK, *Parapholas californica* (Conrad). It is distinguished from other piddocks by scaly overlaping flaps of periostracum on the posterior part of the shell. It bores into soft rocks of the low intertidal and subtidal. Whole specimens are difficult to obtain. Judging from the thick broken shells occasionally washed ashore, they must grow to 150 mm (6") or more.

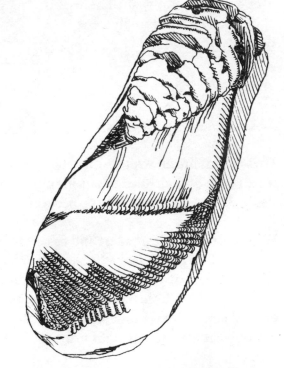

Sometimes we find PIDDOCK CHIMNEYS on the beach. They are cylindrical, 50–70 mm (2 to 3") long, with a round hole at one end and a oval one at the other. They look like they are made out of cement. These line the upper end of the bore hole of the Scale-sided Piddock. They are made partly of lime secreted by the clam, presumably to reinforce the hole.

Scale-sided Piddock

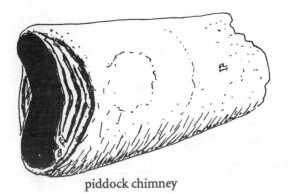

piddock chimney

The WART-NECKED PIDDOCK, *Chaceia ovoidea*
(Gould), 40 mm (1½"), is a chubby species, oval in
outline. It is not too common; and this is about the
northern limit of its range.

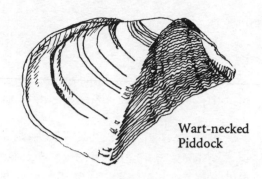

Nearly as small as the Abalone Borer is the BEAKED
PIDDOCK, *Netastoma rostrata* (Valenciennes), 25 mm
(1"). Its shape is hard to explain, but very distinctive. The
posterior end of the shell has a long, slender projection
resembling a bird's beak. Sometimes this projection, called
the siphonoplax, will be bent to one side.

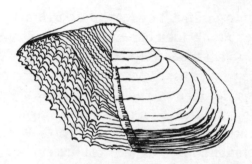

Last is the ROUGH PIDDOCK, *Zirfaea pilsbryi*
Lowe, 80 mm (3"). It is dull white with very rough
ridges along the anterior portion of the shell. It lives
in the thick mud of bays and in soft rocks of
semiprotected coastlines. Common in some areas.

Rough Piddock

SHIPWORMS
Family Teredinidae

The name shipworm is a misnomer. They aren't worms at all, but close relatives of the piddock
clams. Their habit of boring into wood made them the curse of sea captains before the advent of
steel hulls.

Sometimes pieces of wood wash ashore containing the native
SHIPWORM, *Bankia setacea* (Tryon). The shells (and holes) are
usually small, 6 mm (¼"), in diameter, although they reach 20 mm
(¾"). The animal is long and worm-like, much larger than its shell.
An introduced species, *Teredo navalis* Linnaeus, has been reported
from Elkhorn Slough. Even without the shells, a piece of "shipworm wood" makes an interesting addition to the collection.

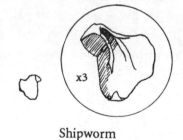

Shipworm

PANDORAS
Family Pandoridae

One of our most unusually shaped bivalves is the DOTTED
PANDORA, *Pandora punctata* Conrad, 35 mm (1⅜"). Its
outline is unmistakable. The valves are nearly flat, dull white on
the exterior, pearly on the interior. It lives offshore, but empty
shells sometimes wash onto the beach.

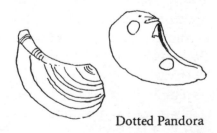

Dotted Pandora

PAPER SHELLS
Family Lyonsiidae

The family Lyonsiidae has three representatives here; one is perhaps the easiest of the clams to identify, and the other two the hardest. All have thin fragile shells.

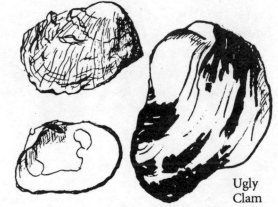

Sea Bottle

The easy one is the SEA BOTTLE, *Mytilimeria nuttalli* Conrad, 25 mm (1"). It is a fragile, bubble-like shell with thin yellow-brown periostracum, and a pearly interior. What makes it easy to recognize is that one finds it, and no other white clam, in globby masses of stiff gelatin-like stuff—sea-squirt (a compound ascidian or tunicate)—which can be whittled off, showing the delicate shell.

The most difficult ones are the parchment clams, and they not only look like each other, but sometimes it's hard to tell them from *Hiatella*. They would be white if they didn't usually wear their wrinkled parchment-like periostracum. The UGLY CLAM, *Entodesma saxicola* (Baird), 50 mm (2"), is a rough-looking character covered with tan or brown wrinkled parchment. It is a fragile shell (except thickened elderly specimens) with a pearly interior. In drying, the skin shrinks and will break the shell unless it has been well oiled.

Ugly
Clam

The CALIFORNIA LYONSIA, *Lyonsia californica* Conrad, 20 mm (¾"), is easily confused with a small *Entodesma*. They both live in the crevices of rocks. Positive distinction between the two can be made by the shape of the muscle scar and pallial line, but in these shells they are usually hard to trace. Ninety-eight out of a hundred parchment clams that you find will be *Entodesma*.

California Lyonsia

LAMP SHELLS
Phylum Brachiopoda

The LAMP SHELL, *Terebratalia transversa* (Sowerby), is not a mollusk at all and usually doesn't appear in shell books. It belongs in an entirely different phylum, the Brachiopoda. However, it has a bivalved shell; there must be many frustrated amateur shell collectors who try to find it in their reference books. It somewhat resembles a flared, curved scallop. The largest I have found is 40 mm (1½") across. It may be white, yellow, pink or orange. The lower valve looks something like a Greek oil lamp. The upper valve has a hollow for the lamp handle to fit into. It lives on rocks in deep water. It is not uncommon on some beaches, but is always a prize find.

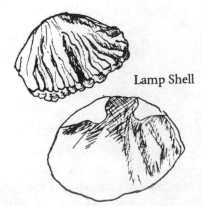

Lamp Shell

PART THREE: CLASS POLYPLACOPHORA

CHITONS
Families Acanthochitonidae, Ischnochitonidae, Callistoplacidae, and Mopaliidae

Chitons (kĭ´-tons) or Coat-of-mail shells, are the little eight-plated, armored ones stuck close to the rocks, and the big leathery ones cast by the dozens onto the beach after storms. They are vegetarians. Chitons must be collected alive if one wants good specimens, because when they die they curl up and can't be straightened without breaking them. As this book is about tide-drift shells, I have included just a few common species which you are likely to *observe* on the rocks. About 30 kinds are known from central California. The little colorful "butterfly shells," their plates, can make a pretty addition to your collection. These are frequently found in the tide drift. Older books place chitons under the class Amphineura.

We'll start with the largest, the big GIANT PACIFIC CHITON, *Cryptochiton stelleri* (Middendorff), 250 mm (10"), family Acanthochitonidae. This really is a giant, the world's largest chiton. I've found them ten inches long and I've heard they get bigger than that. They have a mahogany-colored rough leather on top and their meat looks like abalone. I hear that they were valued as food by the Indians, but I've never tried it. The white plates under the leather girdle are "butterfly shells" and are common in the tide drift. These chitons live in deep water but in the spring we sometimes find them on the low tide rocks.

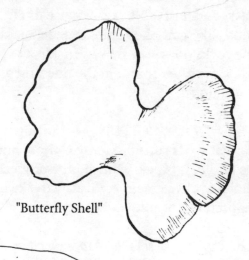

"Butterfly Shell"

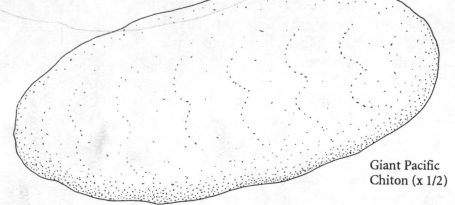

Giant Pacific
Chiton (x 1/2)

We have two common members of the family Ischnochitonidae.

Our very prettiest chiton is the small RED-LINED CHITON, *Tonicella lineata* (Wood), 25 mm (1"), from which come the small red, black, and white striped plates we find in the tide drift. The girdle (the leathery border which holds the plates together) is light brown. This shell lives attached to rocks, just below the sand line at low tide.

Red-lined Chiton

A tiny chiton of this family is GOULD'S BABY CHITON, *Cyanoplax dentiens* (Gould), 10 mm (⅜"), shaped like a tiny Mossy Chiton but without the mossy hairs.

Gould's Baby Chiton

The CALIFORNIA NUTTALL CHITON, *Nuttallina californica* (Reeve), 35 mm (1⅜"), family Callistoplacidae, is a long thin chiton with a few hairs on its dark girdle. The back of the plates are dark but usually eroded light gray. Inside they are pale blue, blue-green, or blue-lavender. The meat is a bright red. They live high on low-tide rocks.

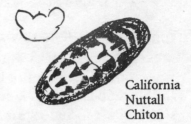

California Nuttall Chiton

I'll mention four chitons of the family Mopaliidae. The most common is probably the MOSSY CHITON, *Mopalia muscosa* (Gould), 50 mm (2"), which we find on the rocks at low tide. It is easy to identify this one because its girdle is covered with stiff moss-like hair like a miniature feather boa. It is grayish-brown like the rocks on which it lives. Inside, the plates are robin's egg blue. They are often found in the tide drift and add a nice color to your collection.

Mossy Chiton

The WOODY CHITON, *Mopalia lignosa* (Gould), 35 mm (1⅜"), is similar to its cousin, Mossy Chiton, but doesn't have the hairs on its girdle. It is pale whitish blue or green inside. The outside of the plates is olive green, vertically streaked with brown and black. An unpretentious but very pretty shell.

Woody Chiton

The HAIRY CHITON, *Mopalia ciliata* (Sowerby), 40 mm (1½"), is very similar outside to Mossy Chiton, but has no mossy fringe. In fact, it takes a magnifying glass to be sure that it has any hairs at all. It is a grayish green outside and whitish inside, sometimes tinted with pink or blue. It is found on the rocks at low tide.

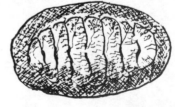

Hairy Chiton

The largest of our chitons, except for the Giant Chiton, is the BLACK KATY, *Katharina tunicata* (Wood), 75 mm (3"). The wide shiny black leathery girdle covers most of the back of the shell. The plates are usually eroded white in the middle, inside they are white. It lives on rocks of the middle tide zone.

Black Katy

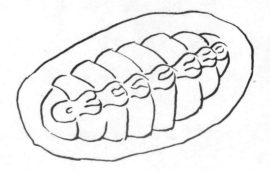

MYSTERIES

Also in my collection are a few shells which don't belong here but that I've found on our beaches. If only I could find them alive instead of dead in the tide drift, then maybe I could discover a range extension. Many are southern California shells which are not supposed to range north of Point Conception. Actually, such finds, even if alive, do not technically constitute range extensions, since there is no proof that there is an established population here. Perhaps the larvae were carried north by currents or on the hulls of boats.

GOULD'S DONAX, *Donax gouldii* Dall, family Donacidae, a small lavenderish clam that shouldn't be north of San Luis Obispo.

Gould's Donax

EASTERN NASSA, *Ilyanassa obsoleta* (Say), family Nassariidae. It is a mudflat scavenger introduced to bays from the East Coast. Why did I find one near Waddell Creek where there are no mudflats? The one I found is shiny brown.

Eastern Nassa

BELCHER'S MUREX, *Forreria belcheri* (Hinds), is a native of southern California and Baja California. One was found at Capitola in 1977. Did it escape from somebody's collection?

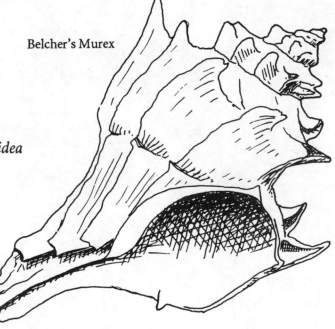

Belcher's Murex

The CALIFORNIA HORN SHELL, *Cerithidea californica*, and the JAPANESE CLAM, *Corbicula manilensis* might also be listed as mysteries. They have already been described.

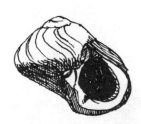

Another southern California shell that has been found, rarely, in Monterey Bay is the NORRIS' TOP SHELL, *Norrisia norrisi* (Sowerby). It is a solid shell, smoother and more squat than our other top shells. A water-worn specimen was collected in 1977 near Santa Cruz by Perry, and a live one was taken many years ago near Monterey according to Smith and Gordon (see references).

Norris' Top Shell

A single valve of *Leporimetis obesa* (Deshayes) was found in 1981 on the beach at Rio del Mar. This member of the tellin family (formerly in the genus *Apolymetis*) ranges from Point Conception to Baja California.

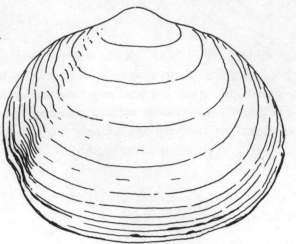

Leporimetis obesa

A HORSE MUSSEL, *Modiolus neglectus* Soot-Ryen, 100 mm (4"), turned up on the mudflats at Elkhorn Slough a few years ago. It has a broadly triangular shape and chestnut-brown periostracum. This species is supposed to live offshore in 15 to 110 meters of water.

Horse Mussel

FURTHER READING

Many of these references will provide further help with identification, while others focus on mollusk habits and life history. Some of these are old friends from my bookshelf which I couldn't resist including, others are newer and in some ways more useful. Some are elementary, others are very technical. Many have extensive bibliographies to lead you, if you so desire, on a merry trail through the literature.

Abbott, R. T. 1974. American seashells. 2nd edition. New York: Van Nostrand Reinhold. 663 p. (Revised edition of a classic work by a famous conchologist)

Abbott, R. T. 1968. Seashells of North America. New York: Golden Press. 280 p. (Especially useful for learning about mollusk families, with examples of species from both coasts)

Arnold, W. H. 1965. A glossary of a thousand-and-one terms used in conchology. The Veliger, vol. 7, supplement. 50 p. (An excellent pamphlet on terminology)

Bernard, F. R. 1983. Catalogue of the living bivalvia of the eastern Pacific Ocean: Bering Strait to Cape Horn. Canadian Special Publication of Fisheries and Aquatic Sciences 61. 192 p. (A technical listing with citations to primary sources)

Cox, K. W. 1962. California abalones, family Haliotidae. California Dept. of Fish and Game, Fish Bulletin No. 118. 133 p. (Includes information on anatomy, identification, natural history, and fisheries)

Fitch, J. E. 1953. Common marine bivalves of California. California Dept. of Fish and Game, Fish Bulletin No. 90. 102 p.

Hanna, G D. 1966. Introduced mollusks of western North America. Occasional Papers of the California Academy of Sciences, no. 48. 108 p. (Includes marine and terrestrial mollusks)

Johnson, M. E., and Snook, H. J. 1927. Seashore animals of the Pacific Coast. New York: Macmillan Company (reprinted in 1967 by Dover Publications). 659 p. (Many of the names have changed, but includes some useful illustrations and information)

Keen, A. M., and Coan, E. 1974. Marine molluscan genera of western North America. Stanford, Calif.: Stanford University Press. 208 p. (A well-illustrated key to genera, with systematic lists, glossary, and a list of ranges and habitats)

Keep, J. 1935. West Coast shells. Revised by J. L. Baily, Jr. Stanford, Calif.: Stanford University Press. 350 p.

Lindberg, D. R. 1981. Acmaeidae (Gastropoda, Mollusca). Pacific Grove, Calif.: The Boxwood Press. 122 p. (Although it focuses on San Francisco Bay, this is the best reference on central California limpets)

McLean, J. H. 1978. Marine shells of southern California. Revised edition. Natural History Museum of Los Angeles County, Science Series no. 24. 104 p. (Includes many species from central California; excellent illustrations and descriptions)

McLean, J. H. 1984. The world of marine micromollusks. Terra, v. 22, no. 6 (July/August), p. 25-30. (A brief introduction to a category of mollusks overlooked in most shell books)

Morris, P. A. 1966. A field guide to the shells of Pacific Coast and Hawaii. Boston: Houghton Mifflin. 297 p. (Of some help, though many of the photos are of poor quality)

Morris, R. H., Abbott, D. P., and Haderlie, E. C., editors. 1980. Intertidal invertebrates of California. Stanford, Calif.: Stanford University Press. 690 p. (A scholarly work, yet very readable and well-illustrated; rich in natural history information and references)

Oldroyd, I. S. 1925–1927. The marine shells of the West Coast of North America. Stanford Univ. Publications in Geological Sciences (2 vols. in 4 parts). (The classic work of its era, but technical with much obsolete nomenclature)

Radwin, G. E., and D'Attilio, A. 1976. Murex shells of the world. Stanford, Calif.: Stanford University Press. 284 p. (Includes California species, color photographs)

Ricketts, E. F., Calvin, Jack, and Hedgpeth, J. W. 1985. Between Pacific tides. 5th edition. Revised by D. W. Phillips. Stanford, Calif.: Stanford University Press. 652 p. (A classic, rich in natural history information on mollusks and other marine life)

Smith, A. G., and Gordon, M. 1948. The marine molluks and brachiopods of Monterey Bay, California, and vicinity. Proceedings of the California Academy of Sciences, 4th series, v. 26, p. 147-245. (Lists 732 species and subspecies; interesting sections on the history of collecting and on fisheries; an important reference, but many of the names have changed)

Smith, R. I., and Carlton, J. T., editors. 1975. Light's manual: intertidal invertebrates of the central California coast. 3rd edition. Berkeley: University of California Press. 716 p. (Keys and systematic lists for nearly all intertidal mollusca in the area covered)

Turgeon, D. D. et al. 1988. Common and scientific names of aquatic invertebrates from the United States and Canada: mollusks. American Fisheries Society Special Publication 16. 277 p. (Proposes standardized common names for mollusks)

We know of no other locality outside of tropical or semitropical areas where the molluscan fauna has such a large number of species [as in Monterey Bay].

Smith and Gordon
1948

INDEX

Abalone Borer, 59
Abalone Worm, 27
Abalones, 16
Acanthina punctulata, 35
    spirata, 35
Acanthochitonidae, 63
Acmaea, 18, 20
Acmaea mitra, 20
Acmaeidae, 18
Acteocina, 40
Acteon punctocaelatus, 40
Acteonidae, 40
Adula californiensis, 44
    falcata, 44
Agate Jewel Box, 48
Alia, 36
Alvinia Shells, 27
Alvinia compacta, 27
Amber Jingle, 47
Amphissa columbiana, 35
    versicolor, 35
Angular Unicorn, 35
Anomia peruviana, 47
Anomiidae, 47
Apolymetis, 66
Apple Seed, 32
Arctic Rock Borer, 59
Astraea gibberosa, 25
Atlantic Slipper, 31

Balcis, 29
Bankia setacea, 61
Barleeia acuta, 27
Barleeia Shells, 27
Barrell Bubble, 40
Batillaria attramentaria, 28
Beaked Piddock, 61
Belcher's Murex, 65
Bent-nose Macoma, 55
Beta Rock Shell, 34
Bittersweet Clams, 42
Bittium attenuatum, 28
    eschrichtii, 28
Black Abalone, 17
Black Katy, 64
Black Tegula, 24
Blue Mussel, 43
Bodega Tellin, 54
Brachiopoda, 62
Broad-winged Scallop, 46
Brown Tegula, 24
Butterfly Shells, 63
Button Shells, 30, 32

California Cone, 39
California Cumingia, 57
California Horn Shell, 28, 65
California Lucine, 48
California Lyonsia, 62
California Mussel, 43
California Nuttall Chiton, 64
California Pea Pod, 44

California Soft-shell Clam, 58
California Trivia, 32
Calliostoma annulatum, 23
    canaliculatum, 23
    gloriosum, 23
    ligatum, 23
    supragranosum, 23
    tricolor, 23
Callistoplacidae, 63, 64
Calyptraeidae, 30
Cancellariidae, 38
Cancellaria cooperi, 38
    crawfordiana, 38
Cardiidae, 52
Carditas, 47
Carditidae, 47
Carinate Chink Shell, 26
Carpenter's Cardita, 47
Carpenter's Dwarf Turban, 25
Carpenter's Horse Mussel, 43
Carpenter's Rock Shell, 34
Ceratostoma foliatum, 33
Cerithidea californica, 28, 65
Cerithiidae, 28
Cerithiopsidae, 28
Cerithiopsis, 28, 29
Chace Wentletrap, 29
Chaceia ovoidea, 61
Chama arcana, 48
    pellucida, 48
Chamidae, 48
Channeled Dog Whelk, 36
Channeled Dogwinkle , 35
Channeled Top, 23
Checked Dog Whelk, 36
Checkered Periwinkle, 26
Chink Shells, 26
Chitons, 63
Chlamys hastata, 46
Chubby Mya, 58
Circled Dwarf Rock Shell, 33
Clinocardium fucanum, 52
    nuttallii, 52
Cockles, 52
Collisella asmi, 21, 24
    digitalis, 18
    instabilis, 20
    limatula, 19
    ochracea, 21
    paradigitalis, 20
    pelta, 19
    scabra, 20
    strigatella, 20
    triangularis, 21
Columbellidae, 35
Columbia Amphissa, 35
Cone Shells, 39
Conidae, 39
Conus californicus, 39
Cooper's Dog Whelk, 37
Cooper's Nutmeg, 38
Corbicula manilensis, 49, 65

Corbiculidae, 49
Crassostrea gigas, 45
Crawford's Nutmeg, 38
Crepidula adunca, 30
    fornicata, 31
    nummaria, 30
    perforans, 30
Crepipatella lingulata, 31
Cryptochiton stelleri, 63
Cryptomya californica, 58
Cumingia californica, 57
Cyanoplax dentiens, 64
Cylichnella culcitella, 40
Cymatiidae, 32
Cystiscus jewettii, 37

Dark Dwarf Turban, 25
Diodora arnoldi, 21
    aspera, 21
Diopatra Worm, 27
Diplodons, 48
Diplodonta orbella, 48
Dish and Surf Clams, 52
Dish Clam, 54
Dog Whelks, 36
Doleful Tower, 39
Donacidae, 65
Donax gouldii, 65
Dotted Pandora, 61
Dove Shells, 35
Dusky Tegula, 24
Dwarf Rock Shells, 33, 34
Dye Shells, 34

Ear Shell, 31
Eastern Nassa, 65
Egregia, 21
Emarginate Dogwinkle, 35
Entodesma saxicola, 62
Epilucina californica, 48
Epitoniidae, 29
Epitonium tinctum, 29
Erato vitellina, 32
Eroded Periwinkle, 26
Erycinidae, 48
Eulimidae, 29

Falcate Date, 44
Fat Dog Whelk, 37
Fenestrate Limpet, 19
File Dwarf Rock Shell, 33
File Limpet, 19
File Shells, 47
Fissurellidae, 18
Flap-tipped Piddock, 60
Flat Abalone, 17
Flat Hoof Shell, 30
Forreria belcheri, 65
Fragile Sphenia, 58
Frilled Dogwinkle, 34
Fucan Cockle, 52
Fusitriton oregonensis, 32

Garden Snail, 41
Gari californica, 56
Gastropoda, 16
Gem Clam, 51
Gemma gemma, 51
Geoduck, 59
Giant Bittium, 28
Giant Keyhole Limpet, 22
Giant Pacific Chiton, 63
Giant Rock Scallop, 46
Glans subquadrata, 47
Glassy Bubble Shells, 40
Glorious Top, 23
Glycymeris subobsoleta, 42
Glycymeridae, 42
Gonyaulax, 43
Gould's Baby Chiton, 64
Gould's Donax, 65
Granula subtrigona, 37
Granulina margaritula, 37
Granulose Top, 23
Grooved Nut, 42

Hairy Chiton, 64
Hairy Triton, 32
Haliotidae, 16
Haliotis assimilis, 17
    corrugata, 17
    cracherodii, 17
    kamtschatkana, 17
    rufescens, 16
    walallensis, 17
Haplotrema sp., 41
Heart Rock-dweller, 52
Helix aspersa, 41
Helminthoglypta cf. *H. nickliniana*, 42
Hiatella, 59, 62
Hiatella arctica, 59
Hiatellidae, 59
Hinnites giganteus, 46
    multirugosus, 46
Hipponicidae, 30
Hipponix cranioides, 30
    serratus, 30
    tumens, 30
Homalopoma carpenteri, 25
    luridum, 25
Honey Dew Limpet, 21
Hooded Keyhole, 22
Hoof Shells, 30
Hooked Slipper, 30
Horn Shells, 28
Horse Mussels, 43, 44, 66

Ida's Miter, 38
Ilyanassa obsoleta, 65
Incised Tower, 39
Indented Macoma, 56
Irus lamellifer, 50
Iris Macoma, 55
Ischnochitonidae, 63, 64
Iselica ovoidea, 40

Jackknife Clam, 56
Japanese Clam, 49, 65
Japanese Littleneck, 51

Japanese Oyster, 45
Jewel Boxes, 48
Jingle Shells, 47
Joseph's Coat, 35

Katharina tunicata, 64
Keeled Doves, 36
Kellia laperousii, 49
Kelliidae, 48, 49
Kelly Shell, 49

Lacuna marmorata, 26
    porrecta, 26
    unifasciata, 26
Lacunidae, 26
Lamellaria rhombica, 31
Lamellariidae, 31
Lamp Shells, 62
Land Snails, 41
Lasaea cistula, 48
    subviridis, 48
Leafy Hornmouth, 33
Lean Dog Whelk, 37
Leporimetis obesa, 66
Leptons, 48
Leptopecten latiauratus, 46
Lewis' Moon Shell, 31
Lima hemphilli, 47
Limaria hemphilli, 47
Limidae, 47
Limpets, 18
Lirularia funiculata, 25
    parcipicta, 25
    succincta, 25
Lirularia Top Shells, 25
Lithophaga plumula, 44
Little Box Lepton, 48
Little Rock Limpet, 21
Little Spotted Dove, 36
Littorina keenae, 26
    planaxis, 26
    scutulata, 26
Littorinidae, 26
Lottia gigantea, 20
Lucines, 48
Lucinidae, 48
Lurid Dwarf Rock Shell, 34
Lyonsia californica, 62

Macoma indentata, 56
    inquinata, 55
    irus, 55
    nasuta, 55
    secta, 55
Mactridae, 52
Mahogany Clam, 56
Margarites pupillus, 24
Marginellas, 37
Marginellidae, 37
Marsh Snails, 41
Mask Limpet, 18
Megasurcula carpenteriana, 39
Megatebennus bimaculatus, 22
Megathura crenulata, 22
Melampidae, 41
Mercenaria mercenaria, 51

Metaxia convexa, 28
Miniature Horn Shells, 28
Minute Pens, 42
Miters, 38
Mitra idae, 38
Mitrella carinata, 36
    gausapata, 36
    tuberosa, 36
Mitridae, 38
Mitromorpha carpenteri, 39
Modest Tellin, 54
Modiolus carpenteri, 43
    flabellatus, 44
    fornicatus, 43
    neglectus, 66
    rectus, 44
Monterey Top, 24
Moon Shells, 31
Mopalia ciliata, 64
    lignosa, 64
    muscosa, 64
Mopaliidae, 63, 64
Mossy Chiton, 64
Murexes, 33
Muricidae, 33
Mussels, 43
Mya arenaria, 58
Myidae, 58
Mytilidae, 43
Mytilimeria nuttalli, 62
Mytilus californianus, 43
    edulis, 43

Nassariidae, 36, 65
Nassarius fossatus, 36
    mendicus, 37
    mendicus cooperi, 37
    perpinguis, 37
    rhinetes, 36
Nassas, 36
Naticidae, 31
Native Oyster, 45
Neat-rib Keyhole Limpet, 21
Netastoma rostrata, 61
Norris' Top Shell, 65
Norrisia norrisi, 65
Notoacmea fenestrata, 19
    insessa, 20, 21
    paleacea, 21
    persona, 18
    scutum, 19
Nucella canaliculata, 35
    emarginata, 35
    lamellosa, 34
Nuculana taphria, 42
Nuculanidae, 42
Nut Clams, 42
Nutmeg Shells, 38
Nuttallia nuttallii, 56
Nuttallina californica, 64
Nuttall's Cockle, 52

Obelisk Shells, 29
Ocenebra atropurpurea, 34
    beta, 34
    circumtexta, 33

foveolata, 33
  interfossa, 34
  lurida, 33, 34
  sclera, 33
Odostomia phanea, 40
Olive Shells, 37
Olivella biplicata, 37
  pycna, 38
Olividae, 37
One-banded Lacuna, 26
Opalia, 29, 34
Opalia chacei, 29
Ophiodermella incisa, 39
Ostrea lurida, 45
Ostreidae, 45
Ovatella myosotis, 41
Owl Limpet, 20
Oysters, 45

Pacific Gaper, 52
Pacific Half Slipper, 31
Pacific Littleneck, 49, 50
Pacific Orb Diplodon, 48
Pacific Spear Scallop, 46
Pandora punctata, 61
Pandoras, 61
Pandoridae, 61
Panopea generosa, 59
Parapholas californica, 60
Pearly Monia, 47
Pectinidae, 45
Pelecypoda, 42
Penitella conradi, 59
  gabbii, 59
  penita, 59, 60
  richardsoni, 59, 60
Petricola carditoides, 52
Petricolidae, 52
Phasianellidae, 25
Pheasant Shells, 25
Pholadidae, 59
Phyllospadix, 21
Phylobrya setosa, 42
Phylobryidae, 42
Piddock Chimneys, 60
Piddocks, 59
Pink Abalone, 17
Pinto Abalone, 17
Pismo Clam, 51
Plate Limpet, 19
Platyodon cancellatus, 58
Pododesmus cepio, 47
Polinices lewisii, 31
Polyplacophora, 63
Potamididae, 28
Prototheca staminea, 49
  staminea ruderata, 50
  tenerrima, 50
Psammobiidae, 56
Pseudomelatoma torosa, 39
Pteropurpura macroptera, 33
Puncturella cucullata, 22
Puppet Margarite, 24
Purple Dwarf Olive, 37
Purple Ringed Top, 23
Pyramid Shells, 40

Pyramidellidae, 40

Quahog, 51

Razor Clams, 57
Red Abalone, 16, 59
Red Turban, 25
Red-lined Chiton, 63
Redwood Snail, 42
Ribbed Finger Limpet, 18
Ribbed Top, 23
Ribbed Venus, 50
Rice Shell, 37
Rictaxis punctocaelatus, 40
Rissoidae, 27
Rock Borer, 44
Rock Dwellers, 52
Rock-dwelling Semele, 57
Rock Shells, 33
Rough Keyhole Limpet, 21
Rough Limpet, 20
Rough Piddock, 61

San Pedro Olive, 38
San Pedro Triphora, 29
Sanguin Clams, 56
Saxicaves, 59
Saxidomus nuttalli, 50
Scale-sided Piddock, 60
Scaled Worm Shell, 27
Scallops, 45
Scaphandridae, 40
Sea Bottle, 62
Sea Buttons, 32
Seaweed Limpet, 20
Seila montereyensis, 28
Semele Clams, 57
Semele rupicola, 57
Semelidae, 57
Serpulorbis squamigerus, 27
Shield Falselimpet, 22
Shield Limpet, 19
Shipworms, 61
Siliqua lucida, 57
  patula, 57
Siphonariidae, 18, 22
Slippers, 30
Small Bubble Shells, 40
Soft-shell Clams, 58
Solenidae, 57
Sphenia fragilis, 58
Spisula catilliformis, 54
Spotted Doves, 36
Spotted Unicorn, 35
Straight Horse Mussel, 44
Striped Barrel Shell, 40
Striped Limpet, 20
Sunset Clam, 56
Surfgrass Limpet, 21

Tagelus californianus, 56
Tapes japonica, 51
Tegula brunnea, 24
  funebralis, 24
  montereyi, 24
  pulligo, 24

Tellina bodegensis, 54
  modesta, 54
Tellinidae, 54, 66
Tellins, 54
Terebratalia transversa, 62
Teredinidae, 61
Teredo navalis, 61
Thaididae, 34
Thais, 34
Thin White Slipper, 30
Thin-shelled Littleneck, 50
Threaded Abalone, 17
Tinted Wentletrap, 29
Tivela stultorum, 51
Tonicella lineata, 63
Top Shells, 23
Tower Shells, 39
Triangular Limpet, 21
Transparent Razor Clam, 57
Tresus capax, 53
  nuttallii, 52, 53
Tri-colored Top, 23
Tricolia pulloides, 25
Trimusculidae, 30
Trimusculus reticulatus, 30, 32
Triphora pedroana, 29
Triphora Shells, 29
Triphoridae, 29
Tritons, 32
Trivia californiana, 32
Triviidae, 32
Trochidae, 23
Turbinidae, 25
Turbonilla, 40
Turridae, 39
Two-spotted Keyhole, 22

Ugly Clam, 62
Ungulinidae, 48
Unstable Limpet, 20

Variegated Chink Shell, 26
Velutina cf. *V. velutina*, 32
Velutinidae, 32
Velvet Shells, 32
Veneridae, 49
Venus Clams, 49
Vermetidae, 27

Wart-necked Piddock, 61
Washington Clam, 50
Wentletraps, 29
Western White Slipper, 30
White Hoof Shell, 30
White Macoma, 55
Whitecap Limpet, 20
Wide-mouthed Snails, 31
Williamia peltoides, 22
Winged Rock Shell, 33
Wood Snail, 41
Woody Chiton, 64
Worm Shells, 27
Yellow Tower, 39

Zirfaea pilsbryi, 61

The author with part of her collection.